MASTER THE™ DSST®

A History
of the

Vietnam War
Exam

About Peterson's®

Peterson's has been your trusted educational publisher for over 50 years. It's a milestone we're quite proud of, as we continue to offer the most accurate, dependable, high-quality educational content in the field, providing you with everything you need to succeed. No matter where you are on your academic or professional path, you can rely on Peterson's for its books, online information, expert test-prep tools, the most up-to-date education exploration data, and the highest quality career success resources—everything you need to achieve your education goals. For our complete line of products, visit **www.petersons.com.**

For more information, contact Peterson's, 4380 S. Syracuse St., Suite 200, Denver, CO 80237; 800-338-3282 Ext. 54229; or visit us online at **www.petersons.com**.

ISBN: 978-0-7689-4455-6

Printed in the United States of America

10 9 8 7 6 5 4 3 2 1   23   22   21

Contents

Before You Begin

HOW THIS BOOK IS ORGANIZED

Peterson's *Master the*™ *DSST® A History of the Vietnam War Exam* provides a diagnostic test, subject-matter review, and a post-test.

- **Diagnostic Test**—Twenty multiple-choice questions, followed by an answer key with detailed answer explanations
- **Assessment Grid**—A chart designed to help you identify areas that you need to focus on based on your test results
- **Subject-Matter Review**—General overview of the exam subject, followed by a review of the relevant topics and terminology covered on the exam
- **Post-test**—Sixty multiple-choice questions, followed by an answer key and detailed answer explanations

The purpose of the diagnostic test is to help you figure out what you know— or don't know. The twenty multiple-choice questions are similar to the ones found on the DSST exam, and they should provide you with a good idea of what to expect. Once you take the diagnostic test, check your answers to see how you did. Included with each correct answer is a brief explanation regarding why a specific answer is correct, and in many cases, why other options are incorrect. Use the assessment grid to identify the questions you miss so that you can spend more time reviewing that information later. As with any exam, knowing your weak spots greatly improves your chances of success.

Following the diagnostic test is a subject-matter review. The review summarizes the various topics covered on the DSST exam. Key terms are defined; important concepts are explained; and when appropriate, examples are provided. As you read the review, some of the information may seem familiar while other information may seem foreign. Again, take note of the unfamiliar because that will most likely cause you problems on the actual exam.

After studying the subject-matter review, you should be ready for the post-test. The post-test contains sixty multiple-choice items, and it will serve as a dry run for the real DSST exam. There are complete answer explanations at the end of the test.

OTHER DSST® PRODUCTS BY PETERSON'S

Books, flashcards, practice tests, and videos available online at **www.petersons.com/testprep/dsst**

- A History of the Vietnam War
- Art of the Western World
- Astronomy
- Business Mathematics
- Business Ethics and Society
- Civil War and Reconstruction
- Computing and Information Technology
- Criminal Justice
- Environmental Science
- Ethics in America
- Ethics in Technology
- Foundations of Education
- Fundamentals of College Algebra
- Fundamentals of Counseling
- Fundamentals of Cybersecurity
- General Anthropology
- Health and Human Development
- History of the Soviet Union
- Human Resource Management

- Introduction to Business
- Introduction to Geography
- Introduction to Geology
- Introduction to Law Enforcement
- Introduction to World Religions
- Lifespan Developmental Psychology
- Math for Liberal Arts
- Management Information Systems
- Money and Banking
- Organizational Behavior
- Personal Finance
- Principles of Advanced English Composition
- Principles of Finance
- Principles of Public Speaking
- Principles of Statistics
- Principles of Supervision
- Substance Abuse
- Technical Writing

Like what you see? Get unlimited access to Peterson's full catalog of DSST practice tests, instructional videos, flashcards, and more for **75% off the first month!** Go to **www.petersons.com/testprep/dsst** and use coupon code **DSST2020** at checkout. Offer expires July 1, 2021.

Chapter 1

All About the DSST® Exam

WHAT IS DSST®?

Previously known as the DANTES Subject Standardized Tests, the DSST program provides the opportunity for individuals to earn college credit for what they have learned outside of the traditional classroom. Accepted or administered at more than 1,900 colleges and universities nationwide and approved by the American Council on Education (ACE), the DSST program enables individuals to use the knowledge they have acquired outside the classroom to accomplish their educational and professional goals.

WHY TAKE A DSST® EXAM?

DSST exams offer a way for you to save both time and money in your quest for a college education. Why enroll in a college course in a subject you already understand? For more than 30 years, the DSST program has offered the perfect solution for individuals who are knowledgeable in a specific subject and want to save both time and money. A passing score on a DSST exam provides physical evidence to universities of proficiency in a specific subject. More than 1,900 accredited and respected colleges and universities across the nation award undergraduate credit for passing scores on DSST exams. With the DSST program, individuals can shave months off the time it takes to earn a degree.

The DSST program offers numerous advantages for individuals in all stages of their educational development:
- Adult learners
- College students
- Military personnel

1

Adult learners desiring college degrees face unique circumstances—demanding work schedules, family responsibilities, and tight budgets. Yet adult learners also have years of valuable work experience that can frequently be applied toward a degree through the DSST program. For example, adult learners with on-the-job experience in business and management might be able to skip the Business 101 courses if they earn passing marks on DSST exams such as Introduction to Business and Principles of Supervision.

Adult learners can put their prior learning into action and move forward with more advanced course work. Adults who have never enrolled in a college course may feel a little uncertain about their abilities. If this describes your situation, then sign up for a DSST exam and see how you do. A passing score may be the boost you need to realize your dream of earning a degree. With family and work commitments, adult learners often feel they lack the time to attend college. The DSST program provides adult learners with the unique opportunity to work toward college degrees without the time constraints of semester-long course work. DSST exams take two hours or less to complete. In one weekend, you could earn credit for multiple college courses.

The DSST exams also benefit students who are already enrolled in a college or university. With college tuition costs on the rise, most students face financial challenges. The fee for each DSST exam starts at $85 (plus administration fees charged by some testing facilities)—significantly less than the $750 average cost of a 3-hour college class. Maximize tuition assistance by taking DSST exams for introductory or mandatory course work. Once you earn a passing score on a DSST exam, you are free to move on to higher-level course work in that subject matter, take desired electives, or focus on courses in a chosen major.

Not only do college students and adult learners profit from DSST exams, but military personnel reap the benefits as well. If you are a member of the armed services at home or abroad, you can initiate your post-military career by taking DSST exams in areas with which you have experience. Military personnel can gain credit anywhere in the world, thanks to the fact that almost all of the tests are available through the internet at designated testing locations. DSST testing facilities are located at more than 500 military installations, so service members on active duty can get a jump-start on a post-military career with the DSST program. As an additional incentive, DANTES (Defense Activity for Non-Traditional Education Support) provides funding for DSST test fees for eligible members of the military.

More than 30 subject-matter tests are available in the fields of Business, Humanities, Math, Physical Science, Social Sciences, and Technology.

Available DSST® Exams	
Business	**Social Sciences**
Business Ethics and Society Business Mathematics Computing and Information Technology Human Resource Management Introduction to Business Management Information Systems Money and Banking Organizational Behavior Personal Finance Principles of Finance Principles of Supervision	A History of the Vietnam War Art of the Western World Criminal Justice Foundations of Education Fundamentals of Counseling General Anthropology History of the Soviet Union Introduction to Geography Introduction to Law Enforcement Lifespan Developmental Psychology Substance Abuse The Civil War and Reconstruction
Humanities	**Physical Sciences**
Ethics in America Introduction to World Religions Principles of Advanced English Composition Principles of Public Speaking	Astronomy Environmental Science Health and Human Development Introduction to Geology
Math	**Technology**
Fundamentals of College Algebra Math for Liberal Arts Principles of Statistics	Ethics in Technology Fundamentals of Cybersecurity Technical Writing

As you can see from the table, the DSST program covers a wide variety of subjects. However, it is important to ask two questions before registering for a DSST exam.

1. Which universities or colleges award credit for passing DSST exams?
2. Which DSST exams are the most relevant to my desired degree and my experience?

Knowing which universities offer DSST credit is important. In all likelihood, a college in your area awards credit for DSST exams, but find out before taking an exam by contacting the university directly. Then review the list of DSST exams to determine which ones are most relevant to the degree you are seeking and to your base of knowledge. Schedule an appointment with your college adviser to determine which exams best fit your degree program and which college courses the DSST exams can replace. Advisers should also be able to tell you the minimum score required on the DSST exam to receive university credit.

DSST® TEST CENTERS

You can find DSST testing locations in community colleges and universities across the country. Check the DSST website (**www.getcollegecredit. com**) for a location near you or contact your local college or university to find out if the school administers DSST exams. Keep in mind that some universities and colleges administer DSST exams only to enrolled students. DSST testing is available to men and women in the armed services at more than 500 military installations around the world.

HOW TO REGISTER FOR A DSST® EXAM

Once you have located a nearby DSST testing facility, you need to contact the testing center to find out the exam administration schedule. Many centers are set up to administer tests via the internet, while others use printed materials. Almost all DSST exams are available as online tests, but the method used depends on the testing center. The cost for each DSST exam starts at $85, and many testing locations charge a fee to cover their costs for administering the tests. Credit cards are the only accepted payment method for taking online DSST exams. Credit card, certified check, and money order are acceptable payment methods for paper-and-pencil tests.

Test takers are allotted two score reports—one mailed to them and another mailed to a designated college or university, if requested. Online tests generate unofficial scores at the end of the test session, while individuals taking paper tests must wait four to six weeks for score reports.

PREPARING FOR A DSST® EXAM

Even though you are knowledgeable in a certain subject matter, you should still prepare for the test to ensure you achieve the highest score possible. The first step in studying for a DSST exam is to find out what will be on the specific test you have chosen. Information regarding test content is located on the DSST fact sheets, which can be downloaded at no cost from **www. getcollegecredit.com**. Each fact sheet outlines the topics covered on a subject-matter test, as well as the approximate percentage assigned to each topic. For example, questions on the A History of the Vietnam War exam are distributed in the following way: 5% on Vietnam before 1940; 9% on World War II, the Cold War, and the first Indochina War; 10% on Diem and nation-state building; 10% on Lyndon Johnson Americanizing the war; 10% on America taking charge; 8% on the home front USA; 9% on Tet; 10% on Vietnamizing the war; 8% on the war at home; 8% on Cambodia and Laos; 8% on the phrase, "A Decent Interval"; and 5% on US legacies and lessons.

In addition to the breakdown of topics on a DSST exam, the fact sheet also lists recommended reference materials. If you do not own the recommended books, then check college bookstores. Avoid paying high prices for new textbooks by looking online for used textbooks. Don't panic if you are unable to locate a specific textbook listed on the fact sheet; the textbooks are merely recommendations. Instead, search for comparable books used in university courses on the specific subject. Current editions are ideal, and it is a good idea to use at least two references when studying for a DSST exam. Of course, the subject matter provided in this book will be a sufficient review for most test takers. However, if you need additional information, it is a good idea to have some of the reference materials at your disposal when preparing for a DSST exam.

Fact sheets include other useful information in addition to a list of reference materials and topics. Each fact sheet includes subject-specific sample questions like those you will encounter on the DSST exam. The sample questions provide an idea of the types of questions you can expect on the exam. Test questions are multiple-choice with one correct answer and three incorrect choices.

The fact sheet also includes information about the number of credit hours ACE has recommended be awarded by colleges for a passing DSST exam score. However, you should keep in mind that not all universities and colleges adhere to the ACE recommendation for DSST credit hours. Some institutions require DSST exam scores higher than the minimum score recommended by ACE. Once you have acquired appropriate reference materials and you have the outline provided on the fact sheet, you are ready to start studying, which is where this book can help.

TEST DAY

After reviewing the material and taking practice tests, you are finally ready to take your DSST exam. Follow these tips for a successful test day experience.

1. **Arrive on time.** Not only is it courteous to arrive on time to the DSST testing facility, but it also allows plenty of time for you to take care of check-in procedures and settle into your surroundings.

2. **Bring identification.** DSST test facilities require that candidates bring a valid government-issued identification card with a current photo and signature. Acceptable forms of identification include a current driver's license, passport, military identification card, or state-issued identification card. Individuals who fail to bring proper identification to the DSST testing facility will not be allowed to take an exam.

3. **Bring the right supplies.** If your exam requires the use of a calculator, you may bring a calculator that meets the specifications. For paper-based exams, you may also bring No. 2 pencils with an eraser and black ballpoint pens. Regardless of the exam methodology, you are NOT allowed to bring reference or study materials, scratch paper, or electronics such as cell phones, personal handheld devices, cameras, alarm wrist watches, or tape recorders to the testing center.

4. **Take the test.** During the exam, take the time to read each question and the provided answers carefully. Eliminate the choices you know are incorrect to narrow the number of potential answers. If a question completely stumps you, take an educated guess and move on—remember that DSSTs are timed; you will have 2 hours to take the exam.

With the proper preparation, DSST exams will save you both time and money. So join the thousands of people who have already reaped the benefits of DSST exams and move closer than ever to your college degree.

A HISTORY OF THE VIETNAM WAR EXAM FACTS

The DSST' A History of the Vietnam War exam consists of 100 multiple-choice questions that assess students for knowledge equivalent to that acquired in a History of the Vietnam War college course. Students have two hours to complete the exam. The exam includes the following topics:

Area or Course Equivalent: A History of the Vietnam War
Level: 3 Lower-level baccalaureate
Amount of Credit: 3 Semester Hours
Minimum Score: 400
Source: https://www.getcollegecredit.com/wp-content/assets/factsheets/AHistoryOfTheVietnamWar.pdf

I. **Vietnam Before 1940 – 5%**
   a. Religious and cultural traditions
   b. Chinese political and cultural domination
   c. A tradition of resistance to invaders
   d. French conquest and colonialism
   e. Development of nationalism and communism
   f. Ho Chi Minh

II. **World War II, the Cold War, and the First Indochina War (1940–1955) – 9%**
   a. Vietnam during World War II
   b. Vietnamese declaration of independence
   c. Restoration of French rule
   d. Global containment
   e. Viet Minh military strategies versus French military strategies
   f. Eisenhower's Vietnam policy
   g. Dien Bien Phu
   h. The Geneva Conference and American response

III. **Diem and Nation-State Building (1955–1963) – 10%**
   a. US support for Diem
   b. Diem's inadequacies
   c. US military and economic assistance

    d. The growing Southern insurgency

    e. JFK's commitment to counter-insurgency

    f. Internal opposition including the Buddhist crisis

    g. The coup against Diem

IV. L.B. Johnson Americanizes the War (1964–1965) – 10%

    a. Political instability in Vietnam

    b. Introduction of the North Vietnamese Army

    c. The Gulf of Tonkin incident and Resolution

    d. The role of Vietnam in the 1964 presidential election

    e. US air campaign over Vietnam: Flaming Dart to Rolling Thunder

    f. Introduction of US combat troops (March through April 1965)

    g. Increase in US combat commitment (July 1965)

V. America Takes Charge (1965–1967) – 10%

    a. Westmoreland's strategy of attrition

    b. Measures of success

    c. The continuing air war

    d. The impact of the war on Vietnamese society

    e. Stabilization of the Saigon regime

    f. America's army in Vietnam

    g. War without fronts: the combat experience

    h. Search and destroy la Drang Valley

VI. Home Front USA (1963–1967) – 8%

    a. The Great Society: guns vs. butter

    b. The credibility gap

    c. Congressional dissent

    d. Television and the press

    e. The civil rights movement

    f. The genesis of the new Left

    g. The draft and draft resistance

VII. Tet (1968) – 9%

    a. Vietnamese planning for the Tet offensive

    b. Communist objectives

    c. The Tet offensive

    d. Reactions in US and Saigon

    e. LBJ decides not to run

    f. Bombing halt and beginning of peace talks

    g. The 1968 election

VIII. Vietnamizing the War (1969–1973) – 10%

    a. Nixon, Kissinger, and Vietnamization

    b. Justifications for Vietnamization (troop withdrawal)

    c. Pacification and the Phoenix Program

    d. My Lai and the deterioration of the US military

    e. Secret negotiations (1969–1971)

    f. The 1972 spring offensive

    g. The October agreement

    h. The Christmas bombing

    i. Triangular diplomacy: the US, the Soviet Union, and China

    j. Paris Peace Accords (1973)

IX. The War at Home (1968–1972) – 8%

    a. Campus unrest

    b. Peace activists and moratoria

    c. The Miami and Chicago conventions

    d. The counterculture, antiwar movement, and silent majority

    e. The Pentagon Papers

X. Cambodia and Laos – 8%

    a. The Geneva Accords (1954)

    b. JFK and Laotian neutrality (1962)

    c. Ho Chi Minh Trail

    d. The secret war in Laos

Chapter 2

A History of the Vietnam War Diagnostic Test

DIAGNOSTIC TEST ANSWER SHEET

1. Ⓐ Ⓑ Ⓒ Ⓓ

2. Ⓐ Ⓑ Ⓒ Ⓓ

3. Ⓐ Ⓑ Ⓒ Ⓓ

4. Ⓐ Ⓑ Ⓒ Ⓓ

5. Ⓐ Ⓑ Ⓒ Ⓓ

6. Ⓐ Ⓑ Ⓒ Ⓓ

7. Ⓐ Ⓑ Ⓒ Ⓓ

8. Ⓐ Ⓑ Ⓒ Ⓓ

9. Ⓐ Ⓑ Ⓒ Ⓓ

10. Ⓐ Ⓑ Ⓒ Ⓓ

11. Ⓐ Ⓑ Ⓒ Ⓓ

12. Ⓐ Ⓑ Ⓒ Ⓓ

13. Ⓐ Ⓑ Ⓒ Ⓓ

14. Ⓐ Ⓑ Ⓒ Ⓓ

15. Ⓐ Ⓑ Ⓒ Ⓓ

16. Ⓐ Ⓑ Ⓒ Ⓓ

17. Ⓐ Ⓑ Ⓒ Ⓓ

18. Ⓐ Ⓑ Ⓒ Ⓓ

19. Ⓐ Ⓑ Ⓒ Ⓓ

20. Ⓐ Ⓑ Ⓒ Ⓓ

A HISTORY OF THE VIETNAM WAR DIAGNOSTIC TEST
24 minutes—20 Questions

Directions: Carefully read each of the following 20 questions. Choose the best answer to each and fill in the corresponding circle on the answer sheet. The Answer Key and Explanations can be found following this Diagnostic Test.

1. The United States supported the presidency of corrupt Vietnamese politician Ngo Ninh Diem because he

   A. used his popularity with the Vietnamese people to urge them to support the United States.
   B. repressed Buddhist monks, many of whom opposed US involvement in Vietnam.
   C. opposed the spread of communism in Asia, which made him useful to the United States.
   D. overthrew puppet ruler Bao Dai to help further the US government's agenda in Vietnam.

2. Which of the following was the term LBJ used to characterize his goals to improve life for Americans?

   A. Head Start
   B. The Great Society
   C. VISTA
   D. The Job Corps

3. Which incident did President Lyndon Johnson use to gain the power to involve the United States in the conflict in Vietnam?

   A. An alleged attack on US ships in the Gulf of Tonkin
   B. Diem's brutal crackdown on Vietnam's Buddhists
   C. The assassination of US president John F. Kennedy
   D. Viet Cong guerilla attacks on Green Beret advisors

4. Which of the following ideas best expresses the desired result of Vietnamization?

A. Americanization

B. Assimilation

C. Escalation

D. Self-sufficiency

5. Which of the following describes the reaction of US and South Vietnamese forces to the Tet Offensive?

A. The shock of the assault routed the South Vietnamese soldiers, who deserted their posts.

B. They overcame their initial surprise and soon detected the enemy's strategic weaknesses.

C. Many demoralized South Vietnamese and American soldiers surrendered to the North Vietnamese insurgents.

D. While fighting off the assault, US troops had to put down a South Vietnamese uprising.

6. Prior to 1940, which foreign power exerted the greatest political and cultural influence over Vietnam?

A. China

B. France

C. Japan

D. India

7. Which of the following did NOT lead to a shift in public opinion regarding support for the war in 1968–1970?

A. Popular author Dr. Benjamin Spock becoming an activist

B. Formation of the Students for a Democratic Society (SDS)

C. Shooting incidents at the Republican Convention in Florida

D. Shooting incidents at universities in Ohio and Florida

8. How did the experience of the Vietnam conflict change American foreign policy?

   A. The US adopted an isolationist policy and avoided foreign wars until the 9/11 attacks.

   B. The US took a proactive stance and negotiated nonaggression clauses in its alliances.

   C. The US granted its State Department veto power as insurance against a recurrence.

   D. The US was reluctant to commit ground troops to foreign wars.

9. How did the operations of the Central Intelligence Agency change during the fighting in Laos?

   A. It operated openly at first, but an attack on its central office made it go underground.

   B. The agency went from being an office that gathered intelligence to a paramilitary training outfit.

   C. It initially reported to the Defense Department but was placed under the control of the US Congress.

   D. It hired only male agents, but it required female agents for its expanding operations.

10. Which global event set the stage for the declaration of Vietnam as an independent democratic republic?

   A. The success of other democratic republics

   B. The establishment of the United Nations

   C. Europe's rebuilding of major urban areas

   D. Japan's defeat at the end of World War II

11. Why did Richard Nixon resign in 1973?

   A. To put the lingering pain of Vietnam to rest by offering the people a symbolic sacrifice.

   B. To avoid impeachment for his role in ordering the Watergate burglary and its cover-up.

   C. To divert attention from the genocide in Cambodia that his military policies had caused.

   D. To meet the terms of a plea agreement to avoid charges in Vice-President Agnew's trial.

12. Senator William Proxmire called for an investigation into the US military action along the Ho Chi Minh Trail because he had been informed of

A. an extensive secret bombing campaign in Laos and Cambodia.

B. a US Air Force scheme to overcharge for bombs it did not it drop.

C. a US Army scheme to break a UN charter granting the Hmong protected status.

D. Nixon having sealed a deal to deliver South Vietnam to the Chinese.

13. Which of the following describes the approach of General William Westmoreland to fighting the war in Vietnam?

A. The military should launch a concentrated offensive with unlimited numbers of US troops.

B. The United States government should use negotiators to help both sides reach a workable compromise.

C. The US Army, Navy, Air Force, and Marine Corps should each focus its might on four different regions.

D. The military should be limited to use of the US Air Force in bombing runs on Viet Cong troops.

14. Which of the Tet Offensive's South Vietnamese targets suffered the most impact?

A. Saigon

B. Haiphong

C. Khe Sanh

D. Hue

15. What was France's response to the Vietnamese declaration of independence?

A. It celebrated Vietnam's example and encouraged its self-rule.

B. It initiated a trade war to destabilize the Vietnamese economy.

C. It declared war on Vietnam and conquered its colony again.

D. It rejected independence efforts and reasserted its dominion.

16. How did the Vietnam experience shape the attitudes of US combat personnel like the Phoenix program's CIA operators and the men of Lieutenant William Calley's Charlie Company?

  A. The constant, oppressive heat of the humid jungles warped the minds of US Army troops.

  B. The US government's focus on body count had become the primary means of measuring success.

  C. Long hours of supervising civilians increased the likelihood of recognizing the humanity in them.

  D. The atmosphere made many soldiers sharper and more able to conduct their operations with cool efficiency.

17. What happened after the United States ended its military involvement in South Vietnam?

  A. The democratic government under President Nguyen Van Thieu brought stability to South Vietnam for four years until communists won control in a national election.

  B. The fighting between north and south continued with South Vietnam gaining territory by using heavy artillery the US military had left behind.

  C. North Vietnam took advantage of the US military pullout by launching a successful offensive that unified Vietnam as a communist state in 1976.

  D. Henry Kissinger guided North Vietnam's government in forging a détente with South Vietnam that helped both countries recover from the war.

18. What was the Ho Chi Minh Trail?

  A. A supply line from North Vietnam to smuggle arms to Viet Cong in the south.

  B. A popular term for Ho's return trip from France to his Vietnamese homeland.

  C. The major highway linking Vietnam's northern highlands to its southern coast.

  D. The training program Vietnamese peasants completed to become Viet Cong.

19. How did US military officials measure the progress their forces made in the Vietnam War?

A. With maps showing how far the enemy forces were driven back.

B. With body counts of how many enemy combatants were killed.

C. By the increasing calls for peace from North Vietnamese officials.

D. By the decreasing population figures for the North Vietnamese.

20. Which issue dominated the 1964 US presidential campaign?

A. Whether the United States needed to conquer Vietnam.

B. The effect of the Vietnam conflict on the US economy.

C. Whether US covert activity should be used in Vietnam.

D. The use of nuclear weapons to settle the Vietnam conflict.

ANSWER KEY AND EXPLANATIONS

1. C	5. B	9. B	13. A	17. C
2. B	6. A	10. D	14. D	18. A
3. A	7. B	11. B	15. D	19. B
4. D	8. D	12. A	16. B	20. D

1. **The correct answer is C.** The US government disliked the way Diem exploited his power but saw him as a means to stabilize Vietnam's government and aid the United States in its fight against communist insurgence. The US did not support Diem's presidency due to his popularity (choice A). In fact, Diem was not popular with his people due to his repressive policies. Choice B doesn't make sense as the Catholic Diem's brutal campaign against Vietnam's Buddhists shocked the world as protesting monks set themselves on fire. Choice D is incorrect because Diem overthrew Emperor Bao Dai to seize power for himself, not to promote US policies in Vietnam.

2. **The correct answer is B.** The Great Society was Johnson's umbrella term for his plan to use legislation and public programs to provide American citizens with opportunities to help them succeed. Head Start (choice A), VISTA (choice C), and the Job Corps (choice D) were programs under Johnson's Great Society plan.

3. **The correct answer is A.** Johnson used reports of a North Vietnamese attack on two US ships in the Gulf of Tonkin to pressure Congress to grant him the power to use US troops in the conflict in Southeast Asia. The cruelty of Diem's treatment of Buddhists created outrage but was not enough to sway Congress into allowing US involvement (choice B). Johnson did not use the assassination of JFK as leverage to enter the fight in Vietnam (choice C). The presence of US Green Berets operating covertly in Vietnam was a secret that Johnson could not expose (choice D).

4. **The correct answer is D.** The idea behind Vietnamization was to make the South Vietnamese accept the responsibility of protecting their nation and train them in the operations of running the war. Americanization (choice A) was the policy under Johnson in which the US ran the military operations in South Vietnam. Assimilation (choice B) is the process of taking on the appearance, behavior, and customs of the people of another culture. Escalation (choice C) is an accelerating increase of an action.

5. **The correct answer is B.** The US and South Vietnamese overcame their surprise and soon detected the enemy's strategic weaknesses. The North Vietnamese devised a plan that had critical oversights, mainly the lack of sufficient troops to mount an assault on the South's military bases, making it marginally easier to drive the communist forces back. Desertion was not a problem faced by the South Vietnamese forces, so choice A doesn't make sense. Choice C can be eliminated because the architects of the Tet Offensive had hoped to demoralize the US and South Vietnamese military, but this did not happen. Choice D can also be eliminated because the offensive was expected to trigger a rebellion among South Vietnamese and that also did not occur.

6. **The correct answer is A.** China, a powerful empire, frequently invaded Southeast Asia. China's domination over the Vietnamese people influenced the region's politics and culture. France (choice B) did not colonize Vietnam until the nineteenth century and impacted the region less than the Chinese had. The same is true of Japan (choice C), which did not focus on Vietnam until the twentieth century. Though it contributed elements of its Hindu culture to Vietnam, the influence of India (choice D) was far less than that of China.

7. **The correct answer is B.** Although the Students for a Democratic Society became involved in the antiwar effort by the mid-1960s, this group originally formed as part of the civil rights movement in 1959. The formation of the SDS did not lead to shift in public opinion regarding support for the war in 1968–1970 as much as the activism of Dr. Spock (choice A), the shooting incidents at the Republican Convention in Florida (choice C), or the shooting incidents at universities in Ohio and Florida (choice D).

8. The correct answer is D. Following the US involvement in the conflict in Vietnam, the United States developed what has been called "Vietnam Syndrome"—a new risk-adverse policy regarding foreign wars, which included a reluctance to commit ground troops in order to minimize American casualties. This new reluctance did not mean that all foreign wars were avoided entirely until 9/11 (choice A), as evidenced in the US involvement in the Persian Gulf, Iraq, and Afghanistan. The Vietnam conflict did not lead to renegotiating nonaggression clauses (choice B) or grant the State Department veto power as insurance against a recurrence similar to the Vietnam conflict (choice C).

9. The correct answer is B. Originally, the CIA focused on gathering information and analyzing it, but teaching the Hmong people military tactics transformed the agency into a paramilitary training academy. Choice A is incorrect because the CIA had always operated secretly. The change did not involve answering to a different entity (choice C) or modify its hiring policies (choice D).

10. The correct answer is D. The fall of Japan led to the Japanese retreat from Japanese-occupied Vietnam, creating a political vacuum that permitted the Viet Minh to seize power. The establishment of successful democracies elsewhere (choice A) had no effect on the exchange of power in Vietnam. The establishment of the United Nations (choice B) had no effect on the exchange of power either. The rebuilding of major European urban centers (choice C) had no influence over Southeast Asian affairs.

11. The correct answer is B. President Nixon resigned in order to avoid the public humiliation of a trial in the Senate for his criminal acts and being turned out of the White House in disgrace. His reasons for resigning were not meant to offer a symbolic sacrifice to the American people (choice A). Rather than expressing humility, Nixon remained defiant in the face of leaving Washington. Choice C is incorrect because the Cambodian genocide had not yet begun and would be unknown to the outside world until 1978. Nixon's departure was not part of a plea agreement to avoid being named as an accessory in his vice president's bribery trial (choice D).

12. **The correct answer is A.** An informant told Proxmire that Nixon secretly ordered an extensive bombing campaign over Laos and Cambodia that included carpet and cluster bombing. Proxmire had no suspicions about military fraud (choice B), UN charter violations (choice C), or a secret deal to sell out South Vietnam (choice D).

13. **The correct answer is A.** General Westmoreland was a war hawk who believed in using the full power of the US military to crush the enemy, a feat that would require a huge expenditure of arms and personnel. He did not believe in negotiation as a viable tool in ending the conflict in Vietnam (choice B). Choice C is incorrect because he deployed US forces throughout Southeast Asia where they worked together as needed to support various offensives. Choice D is incorrect because the sole use of the US Air Force was not a consideration.

14. **The correct answer is D.** The North Vietnamese communist forces launched a three-week-long assault on the large city of Hue and massacred 5,000 of its civilian residents. The impact of the offensive in Saigon (choice A) was largely psychological as news photos showed the enemy engaging in combat within the courtyard of the United States Embassy, which made the US military look weak. Haiphong (choice B) is a city located in North Vietnam, not South Vietnam. Khe Sanh (choice C) was the first target of North Vietnamese forces in which they staged a firefight to serve as a diversion to keep South Vietnamese forces away from areas where North Vietnamese forces were making preparations for the offensive.

15. **The correct answer is D.** France refused to recognize the independence of Vietnam and sought to reassert its power over the Southeast Asian colony. France did not embrace the efforts of Vietnam to establish itself as an independent nation (choice A). It also did not retaliate by commencing a trade war with the intention of ruining Vietnam's economy (choice B). Choice C is incorrect because France fought the Viet Minh rebellion but could not recapture its entire former territory, only retaking the southern half of Vietnam.

16. **The correct answer is B.** Because the US did not intend to occupy North Vietnam, it relied on high body counts (rather than on maps defining territory won and lost) to measure success. However, because many Viet Cong did not wear uniforms, dead civilians could easily be included in the body counts. In addition, the Viet Cong sometimes used civilians, including women and children, to deliver grenades. These factors contributed to a negative change in attitudes towards Vietnamese civilians, which in part fueled war atrocities like My Lai and the horrors of the Phoenix program. While choice A may be true, it is not the best answer because when stresses like heat drive someone to snap, the short eruption of violence it produces is not as methodical as was seen at My Lai and in the Phoenix Program. Choice C is incorrect because rather than increasing the perceived humanity of other people, the long hours generally led to the opposite. The tense environment may have sharpened the senses of some soldiers, but this has no bearing on their willingness to commit atrocities in the name of following orders (choice D).

17. **The correct answer is C.** Despite the effort expended under the Vietnamization policy, the South Vietnamese Army never became a formidable fighting force and was left in a weakened condition following the US military pullout. North Vietnam took advantage of the US military pullout by launching a successful offensive that unified Vietnam as a communist state in 1976. The scenarios presented in choices A, B, and D are false.

18. **The correct answer is A.** The Ho Chi Minh Trail was a meandering route from North Vietnam through the adjoining regions of Cambodia and Laos into South Vietnam. It was used as a supply line to smuggle arms to the Viet Cong fighting in the south. It did not describe the return route of Ho from France to North Vietnam (choice B). The trail was not a major highway running through Vietnam from north to south (choice C). Choice D is incorrect because the Viet Cong had no formal training program to train soldiers. The brief instruction peasants received was backed up by advice from other Viet Cong members and personal experience.

19. **The correct answer is B.** Following a battle, US forces searched the area and counted the number of enemy dead, figures which very often were inaccurate or inflated. Mapping the progress (choice A) did little good as regions could not be permanently cleared of the enemy, who surfaced again later (choice A). North Vietnamese officials did not attempt to negotiate a peace with the US military (choice C). North Vietnam did not tabulate and report their population figures during the conflict (choice D).

20. **The correct answer is D.** Johnson's opponent, Senator Barry Goldwater, was a war hawk who wanted to use the H-bomb to end the conflict in Vietnam. Johnson in turn hired US advertising experts to design compelling campaign ads that touched on the public's fear of nuclear war. Conquest of Vietnam (choice A) was not on the table, as the United States had no desire to engage in imperialism. Choice B is incorrect because the conflict in Vietnam had not affected the US economy significantly during the campaign. The use of US covert activity in Vietnam (choice C) was already occurring but was not mentioned publicly, so it was not an issue during the campaign.

DIAGNOSTIC TEST ASSESSMENT GRID

Now that you've completed the diagnostic test and read through the answer explanations, you can use your results to focus your studying. Find the question numbers from the diagnostic test that you answered incorrectly and highlight or circle them below. Then, focus extra attention on the sections within Chapter 3 dealing with those topics.

A History of the Vietnam War		
Content Area	**Topic**	**Question #**
Vietnam Before 1940	• Religious and cultural traditions • Chinese political and cultural domination • A tradition of resistance to invaders • French conquest and colonialism • Development of nationalism and communism • Ho Chi Minh	6
World War II, the Cold War, and the First Indochina War (1940–1955)	• Vietnam during World War II • Vietnamese Declaration of Independence-Global containment • Viet Minh military strategies versus French military strategies • Eisenhower's Vietnam policy • Dien Bien Phu • The Geneva Conference and American response	10, 15
Diem and Nation-State Building (1955–1963)	• US support for Diem • Diem's inadequacies • US military and economic assistance • The growing Southern insurgency • JFK's commitment to counterinsurgency • Internal opposition including the Buddhist crisis • The coup against Diem	1, 18
L.B. Johnson Americanizes the War (1964–1965)	• Political instability in Vietnam • Introduction of the North Vietnamese Army • The Gulf of Tonkin incident and Resolution • The role of Vietnam in the 1964 presidential campaign • US air campaign over Vietnam: Flaming Dart to Rolling Thunder • Introduction of US combat troops (March through April 1965) • Increase in US combat commitment (July 1965)	3, 20

A History of the Vietnam War

Content Area	Topic	Question #
America Takes Charge (1965–1967)	• Westmoreland's strategy of attrition • Measures of success • The continuing air war • The impact of the war on Vietnamese society • Stabilization of the Saigon regime • America's army in Vietnam • War without fronts: the combat experience • Search and destroy Ia Drang Valley	13, 19
Home Front USA (1963–1967)	• The Great Society: guns vs. butter • The credibility gap • Congressional dissent • Television and the press • The civil rights movement • The genesis of the New Left • The draft and draft resistance	2
Tet (1968)	• Vietnamese planning for the Tet offensive • Communist objectives • The Tet offensive • Reactions in US and Saigon • LBJ decides not to run • Bombing halt and the beginning of peace talks • The 1968 election	5, 14
Vietnamizing the War (1969–1973)	• Nixon, Kissinger, and Vietnamization • Justifications for Vietnamization (troop withdrawal) • Pacification and the Phoenix program • My Lai and the deterioration of the US military • Secret Negotiations (1969–1971) • The 1972 Spring offensive • The October agreement • The Christmas bombing • Triangular diplomacy: The US, the Soviet Union, and China • Paris Peace Accords (1973)	4, 16

A History of the Vietnam War

Content Area	Topic	Question #
The War at Home (1968–1972)	• Campus unrest • Peace activists and moratoria • The Miami and Chicago conventions • The counterculture, antiwar movement, and silent majority • The Pentagon Papers	7
Cambodia and Laos	• The Geneva Accords • JFK and Laotian neutrality • Ho Chi Minh Trail • The secret war in Laos • Sihanouk and Cambodia's neutrality • Lon Nol and the US incursion • The secret bombing of Laos and Cambodia • The Khmer Rouge and the fall of Phnom Penh (1975) • The communist victory in Laos	9, 12
"A Decent Interval"	• The cease-fire violations • Watergate and Nixon's resignation • Congressional passage of the War Powers Act • The Great Spring Offensive • The fall of Saigon	11, 17
US Legacies and Lessons	• Impact of the war on Vietnam • The impact of the Vietnam Syndrome on American foreign policy • The experience of returning vets • Economic consequences • The impact on the US military • The impact on the media • POWs and MIAs • Collective national amnesia	8

Chapter 3

A History of the Vietnam War Subject Review

OVERVIEW

- **Vietnam Before 1940**
- **World War II, the Cold War, and the First Indochina War (1940–1955)**
- **Diem and Nation-State Building (1955–1963)**
- **Lyndon B. Johnson Americanizes the War (1964–1965)**
- **America Takes Charge (1965–1967)**
- **Home Front USA (1963–1967)**
- **Tet (1968)**
- **Vietnamizing the War (1969–1973)**
- **The War at Home (1968–1972)**
- **Cambodia and Laos**
- **"A Decent Interval"**
- **US Legacies and Lessons**
- **Summing It Up**

Of all the wars the United States has fought, Vietnam may be one of the most impactful to American society, both civilian and military. From deceptions perpetrated at the highest level to guerilla warfare and a collapse of order within the ranks of the military, no war, except the Civil War, has both unified and divided the nation. Like the Civil War, the effect of the Vietnam War on our society can still be felt, almost 50 years later.

VIETNAM BEFORE 1940

Religious and Cultural Traditions

Stretching along the Pacific coast of Southeast Asia, Vietnam encompasses approximately 331,212 km^2 (127,882 sq. mi.). Throughout its long history, this small nation has been home to dozens of different ethnic and cultural groups. Humans have inhabited the region for nearly 500,000 years. Around 1000 BCE, wet rice cultivation began and became the foundation of Vietnam's earliest civilizations. The Vietnamese people consider themselves fiercely independent. For more than 2,000 years, they fought off invaders and colonizers from both China and Europe to create their own nation. The mix of these different influences has helped create unique cultural and religious traditions.

China has exercised the greatest influence over Vietnamese culture, but the Vietnamese have also incorporated elements of Hindu culture from South Asia and French culture from Europe. In addition, there are several major indigenous groups like the Khmer in southwestern Vietnam and the Hmong from the mountainous regions of the north. The main language is Vietnamese. Many people in the country also speak Chinese, French, and English as second languages.

The Chinese brought Confucianism and Daoism to Vietnam. Considered both a religion and a philosophy, **Confucianism** emphasizes rational thought and respect for historical traditions. **Daoism** focuses on a sense of harmony between humans and nature. Confucianism and Daoism were strongest in the north. **Buddhism**, which originated in India, is the single largest religion in Vietnam. Buddhists follow the teachings of Siddhartha Gautama, the Buddha, who preached that people could reach enlightenment through study and meditation. French colonization introduced Catholicism, predominately in the south. Catholics are the largest Christian group in Vietnam. All these religions, however, are infused with local and indigenous traditions.

Tet, the Vietnamese New Year, is based on the lunar calendar. Tet is the most important holiday, unifying people of all religions and ethnic groups in Vietnam. The festival lasts several days and provides an opportunity for families to gather to honor their ancestors. Other holidays include a Lantern Festival similar to the Chinese New Year, and the autumn harvest festival of Tet Trung Thu. Folk beliefs in Vietnam often take the form of

animism, the idea that plants, animals, and all natural entities possess a living spirit. Traditional rituals invoke these spirits to insure the health and wellbeing of the family and community. The family is the center of Vietnamese cultural life, and local ritual and traditions reinforce and strengthen family ties.

Chinese Political and Cultural Domination

Around 179 BCE, China first gained control of Vietnam when a Chinese warlord invaded the indigenous kingdoms of Lac Viet and Au Viet. By 111 BCE, China's Han Dynasty had cemented control over the region. For the next thousand years, China ruled Vietnam, bringing their language, technology, and system of government. China introduced literacy with its written language. The Vietnamese language did not have its own written alphabet until Portuguese missionaries developed one in the seventeenth century. Still, Chinese remained the primary written language of all literary works and legal documents in Vietnam until the 20th century. The Chinese brought improved methods of irrigation and superior metalworking techniques. The introduction of metal plows and domesticated animals like pigs and water buffalo transformed agriculture. The Vietnamese also learned from Chinese tradesmen how to produce high-quality pottery.

Initially, the Chinese were not completely autocratic in their rule. Although a Chinese governor oversaw each province in Vietnam, lesser officials came from the local aristocracy, allowing Vietnam a certain degree of home rule. However, around 100 BCE, when the Han Dynasty began to expand, China sought greater control over the country. Vietnam's rich soil along the Red River Delta and its ports on the South China Sea made it an essential part of China's growing empire in Asia. Chinese rulers in Vietnam started to promote Chinese customs, religion, and language more aggressively. Known as **sinicization**, this process of influencing and adapting a nontraditional Chinese culture to the Chinese way of life often came at the point of a spear. Those who persisted in practicing local traditions and speaking indigenous languages could be fined, imprisoned or, in some cases, put to death. This approach generated hostility and rebellion among the Vietnamese. Even those who were well integrated into Chinese society did not identify as fully Chinese. The Chinese left an indelible stamp on Vietnamese culture, yet they also spurred a tradition of independence that became crucial to the nation's later development.

A Tradition of Resistance to Invaders

In 40 CE, two sisters from a wealthy family launched the first major rebellion against the Chinese. Tru'ng Trac and Tru'ng Nhi had received an unusual education for women at that time. Because their father had no sons, he taught them martial arts, literature, politics, and history. Like many Vietnamese, the sisters objected to the brutal tactics of the Han Dynasty. After assembling a sizable army, the Tru'ng sisters drove the Chinese from their village. By 43 CE, they had freed their province of Nanyue from Han rule and declared themselves joint queens of the region. According to legend, their army consisted largely of women, though this has never been historically verified. The reign of the Tru'ngs proved short lived. The Chinese emperor dispatched general Ma Yuan to quell the uprising. In 43 CE, the general routed the sisters in battle. The sisters later died, either by suicide or execution. Though their rebellion ultimately failed, the Tru'ng sisters became legendary figures in Vietnam's history. They are honored to the present day.

Chinese rule returned to Vietnam and continued for most of the next five centuries. Occasional insurrections sprang up. In 225 CE, the aristocratic Lady Triue led a rebellion that endured for more than twenty years, until the Chinese quashed it in 248 CE. Between 544 and 604 CE, the rebel leader Ly Bon established the Ly Dynasty and ruled over an independent kingdom called **Van Xuan** in the northern region. Once more, the Chinese reasserted their power, and Vietnam remained under Chinese rule from 604 until 939 CE when Ngo Quyen of Gaio Chau province in northern Vietnam finally drove the Chinese out and unified Vietnam into a single kingdom called **Nam Viet**. For over nine centuries, Vietnam maintained its independence from foreign rule. During that time, the nation repelled several invasions by the Chinese and Mongols.

The Vietnamese utilized the skills they had learned under the Chinese. Education, healthcare, engineering, and legal studies flourished in the kingdom. Vietnam developed one of the most advanced civilizations in Southeast Asia.

In 1516, the first European contact came with the arrival of Portuguese explorers, followed by the Dutch. By that time, the Vietnamese rulers had become so secure and powerful that the Europeans saw little chance of colonizing the land. The Vietnamese were happy to trade with the Europeans but did not allow permanent European outposts on their territory. However, Catholic missionaries were tolerated but not encouraged. Many

Vietnamese perceived Christianity as having a weakening effect on Vietnamese traditions. During the first half of the nineteenth century under the Nguyen Dynasty, Vietnam became increasingly hostile to outsiders. The government persecuted missionaries and Catholic converts and sought to limit trade with European merchants. The suppression of trade weakened the economy and led to a series of revolts.

French Conquest and Colonialism

France saw Vietnam's growing political and economic instability as an opportunity to expand its colonial empire in Southeast Asia. In 1858, the French Navy attacked the port city of Da Nang. Over the next eight years, the French established a foothold in the Mekong Delta. Fierce resistance from the Vietnamese made colonization a slow process. It took another twenty years for France to defeat Vietnam. In 1887, France finally declared Vietnam to be French Indochina.

The French established a plantation system to exploit Vietnam's agricultural products. Farmers grew cash crops like rice, tea, coffee, spices, and rubber under the supervision of French landowners who exported the crops to Europe. Coal, tin, zinc, and timber also enriched French coffers. The French government constructed a network of railroads to transport goods to the ports. The railroads also made it possible to connect people living in remote provinces to create a more unified Vietnam.

Under French rule, Saigon became a leading center of culture, as well as trade, in South Vietnam. The French brought their language, religion, culture, and architecture. Opera houses, theaters, cafes, and wide boulevards reflected the Beaux Arts style popular in Europe during the last half of the nineteenth century. The French transformed Saigon into the so-called "Paris of Indochina." The French controlled Vietnam until 1954. The Vietnamese, however, never acquiesced entirely to French rule. The French colonial era saw frequent uprisings and nationalist movements as Vietnam once more sought to assert its independence.

Development of Nationalism and Communism

During the early twentieth century, the European-educated Vietnamese youth began to form political movements that challenged French authority. Some of them turned to Japan for help and military support. Japan was one of the few nations in Asia that had successfully avoided being fully colonized by Western empires. As such, anticolonialists looked to Japan as a model for Vietnam. In 1904, a village schoolteacher's son named Phan Boi Chau founded Vietnam's first nationalist party, the **Vietnam Modernization Association**. Phan had delved into both Confucianism and European philosophy. Even as a young man, he was drawn to resistance movements. Phan drew up a three-point plan to overthrow French rule. His plan included seeking assistance from Japan. The Japanese, however, were reluctant to become involved in French-Vietnamese politics. Without aid from Japan, the Vietnam Modernization Association lacked the power to rout the colonists. French authorities used force to put down the resistance movement, arresting, imprisoning, or executing thousands of activists. In 1909, Phan went into exile in Hong Kong, and his association disbanded.

Three years later in 1912, Phan returned to Vietnam to help establish the **Vietnam Restoration Society**. While the Modernization Association had assumed that Vietnam's traditional monarchy would return to power once the French left, the Restoration Society openly advocated democracy. It was the first major movement in Vietnam to do so. The Restoration Society launched a series of armed uprisings but failed to dislodge the French. From his exile in China, Phan briefly organized a nationalist government, but the French pushed the Chinese to arrest him and his followers. Phan spent the rest of his life in prison or exile. In 1925, the French placed him under house arrest. Phan Boi Chau died in 1940.

The impetus for independence, however, continued to gain traction. Revolutionary movements in Russia and China drew Vietnamese intellectuals to socialism and communism. In 1925, Nguyen Ai Quoc organized the **Revolutionary Youth League**, which became the Vietnamese Communist Party five years later. Nguyen Ai Quoc later would change his name to Ho Chi Minh.

Ho Chi Minh

Ho Chi Minh was born in 1890. In 1911, Ho left Vietnam to work as a French seaman. His interest in anti-imperialism and politics formed early in life when his father, a local official, had refused to work for the French colonial government. Ho's province had been the site of many nationalist rebellions. After leaving Vietnam, Ho spent fourteen years traveling through Europe and the United States. In 1920, he helped found the French Communist Party. Communists objected to private property and capitalism, believing that all land and means of production should be in the hands of the workers. Ho saw communism as a form of anti-imperialism. He considered how a communist movement in Vietnam could rally the peasants to throw off French rule. In 1923, Ho studied in Moscow with an organization known as the Comintern, the international wing of the Communist Party. In 1917, after Russia's communist revolution, the Russian leader Nikolai Lenin had established the Comintern to educate potential leaders for a worldwide communist revolution.

After his sojourn in Moscow, Ho traveled to China where he became active among Vietnamese political exiles. Both the Revolutionary Youth League and the Vietnamese Communist Party were originally established in China. Throughout the 1930s, Ho continued to travel between Russia and China, building support for his movement.

In 1940, Japan invaded Vietnam and Indochina. Ho returned to Vietnam and organized the **Viet Minh**, a communist guerilla group, to fight the Japanese. Ho believed that fighting alongside the French and Allies during World War II would convince the French to grant the Vietnamese independence. The French, however, had little intention of relinquishing the last vestiges of their empire.

WORLD WAR II, THE COLD WAR, AND THE FIRST INDOCHINA WAR (1940–1955)

Vietnam during World War II

In September 1940, Japan seized control of French Indochina. Since France had already surrendered to Nazi Germany, the French forces put up little resistance. The French signed a treaty with Japan that allowed French officials to administer Indochina as a puppet state under the authority of Vichy France. Dominance over Indochina was crucial to Japan's war plan. Once Japan subdued Indochina, the Japanese could use it a base for their campaign to conquer Asia and the Pacific.

The Viet Minh, under the leadership of Ho Chi Minh, led the Vietnamese resistance against the Japanese occupation. Viet Minh fighters worked with British and American troops to provide military intelligence on Japanese movements in the region. The Viet Minh (translated as the League for Independence of Vietnam) was predominantly communist, but it also brought together several other nationalist factions.

The Vietnamese people suffered greatly under the Japanese occupation. Widespread famine, brought on in part by Japanese policies, drained Vietnam economically and led to millions of deaths.

Vietnamese Declaration of Independence

Ho Chi Minh hoped that the Viet Minh would win recognition from the Allies as the legitimate government of Vietnam once the Japanese had been defeated. In August 1945, that goal seemed near when the Japanese surrendered. Amid the chaos of the Japanese withdrawal, Ho Chi Minh and his Viet Minh seized power, declaring the country the Democratic Republic of Vietnam. Despite its name, the new government was communist controlled. The Vietnamese emperor, Bao Dai, abdicated his throne in favor of the republic. Bao, of the Nguyen Dynasty, would be the last emperor of Vietnam.

Restoration of French Rule

France refused to recognize Vietnam's independence. With the aid of the British in 1946, French forces took control of the south, effectively creating two Vietnams: Communist-controlled North Vietnam and noncommunist South Vietnam. Meanwhile, Ho Chi Minh was struggling to maintain control of his coalition. The end of World War II had freed various nationalist groups from their loyalty to the Viet Minh. Without a common enemy, these factions lacked a reason to unify. Chinese-backed nationalist groups in particular, threatened the autonomy of North Vietnam.

Neither the French nor the Viet Minh wanted to see China expand its influence. Faced with a common enemy, both sides attempted a negotiated truce in March 1946. The French would remain in control of South Vietnam and withdraw their troops over a period of five years. An independent Vietnam would then become part of the French Union, a loose alliance of France and its former colonies similar to the British Commonwealth. The French would also help the Viet Minh repel Chinese-backed groups. The arrangement proved short lived. As its imperial empire disintegrated in the aftermath of World War II, France clung more strongly than ever to its remaining colonies in Indochina. Rather than withdraw, France established its own republic in Cochinchina, an Indochinese region that encompassed most of Vietnam including the city of Saigon. The republic was actually a French colony. The Viet Minh objected. The French attacked the port city of Haiphong in northeastern Vietnam, causing enormous civilian casualties. Viet Minh and French troops engaged in battle in Hanoi. By the end of 1946, the First Indochina War had begun. It would last until 1955.

Global Containment

After World War II, the balance of world power realigned between communism and western-style democracy. The United States emerged as the leader of the western world. The Soviet Union controlled the communist bloc in Eastern Europe. In 1949, China became communist and took the name the People's Republic of China. Though during the Cold War the United States never engaged directly with either the Soviet Union or China, there were several indirect conflicts, or proxy-wars.

The United States subscribed to the **domino theory**, which was the belief that if one country fell to communism, the surrounding countries would soon follow. Since the US and its allies could not eliminate communism, they believed they could contain it by suppressing communist movements in independent nations. **Global containment** meant that communism would stay mostly to the Soviet eastern-bloc countries and China. Anti-communism was a linchpin of American foreign policy. The United States provided aid to the French, though that aid stopped short of sending US troops. Still, US investment in the French-Viet Minh conflict paved the way for the later war between the United States and North Vietnam.

Viet Minh Military Strategies versus French Military Strategies

The **First Indochina War** became a confrontation between a foreign army with traditional training and local guerilla forces. The French were better armed, better trained, and more disciplined than the Viet Minh. The French also had air power and could bomb cites and ports. In contrast, the Viet Minh had only what guns they could take from retreating Japanese or from French prisoners. There were few planes, and the volunteers had little military experience. While the Viet Minh did outnumber the French forces, this was not an initial advantage. The French used their superior weapons to consolidate their territory. By 1949, the French took control of most of Vietnam, declared the country the Associated State of Vietnam, and reinstalled the former emperor Bao Dai as a French puppet leader.

The Viet Minh, however, refused to surrender. Under the leadership of General Vo Nguyen Giap, they became experts in guerilla warfare. Giap

modeled his strategy on that of Mao Zedong of China, who had used guerilla tactics during his successful communist revolution in China. The Viet
Minh relied on small bands of insurgents to attack French bases and then
withdraw into the countryside where they would blend in with the local
population. The Viet Minh avoided large-scale battles, preferring to sud-
denly strike the enemy and inflict as much damage as possible as quickly as
possible. Guerilla forces did not recognize formal borders between French
and Viet Minh territory, so the French had no idea when and where the
guerillas might strike next. By the early 1950s, the Viet Minh had begun to
wear the French military down.

Eisenhower's Vietnam Policy

US President Dwight D. Eisenhower opposed the spread of communism,
but he was cautious about committing troops to Vietnam. Eisenhower did
not endorse French colonialism, though he provided weapons and other
military aid to the French. The United States also assisted the French finan-
cially and underwrote much of the cost of the war. Overall, Eisenhower
wanted to avoid engaging directly with the Viet Minh. He did, however,
use the Central Intelligence Agency (CIA) to help place Ngo Dinh Diem in
power as the president of South Vietnam. US involvement increased after
the Battle of Dien Bien Phu, but the French could not hold the region. Some
historians feel that earlier and more vigorous intervention may have pre-
vented the later war, though this is debatable. Eisenhower's policy was in
keeping with the feelings of most Americans at that time. Following World
War II, the United States had emerged a strong victor with a booming
economy. Americans wanted to avoid prolonged foreign conflicts and focus
on domestic growth at home.

Dien Bien Phu

Dien Bien Phu proved the most decisive battle in the First Indochina War.
In late 1953, French forces seized Dien Bien Phu, a valley located on the
border between Vietnam and Laos. Vietnamese nationalists used roads
through the valley to transport soldiers and supplies. The French had failed
to make significant gains against the Viet Minh. They hoped that control
over the valley would give them a base from which to extend their hold over
Indochina. In March 1954, the Viet Minh attacked. They used weapons

supplied by the Chinese. The Vietnamese forces took the French by surprise and overwhelmed them. On May 7, the Viet Minh finally pushed the French from their stronghold. Dien Bien Phu was in the hands of the Vietnamese. The Viet Minh victory marked the end of French influence in Indochina. Conceding defeat, the French indicated they were ready to sign a peace settlement with the Viet Minh and withdraw from the region.

The Geneva Conference and American Response

Between April 26 and July 21, 1954, representatives from nine countries met in Geneva, Switzerland, to draw up a plan for peace in Vietnam. Those nations were France, the United States, Great Britain, the Soviet Union, the People's Republic of China, Laos, Cambodia, North Vietnam (the Viet Minh), and South Vietnam (the State of Vietnam). North and South Vietnam attended the conference as separate entities. The conference, known as the **Geneva Accords**, drafted a series of agreements and a document called the **Final Declaration**. The declaration's goal was to ultimately unify Vietnam under a freely elected government.

The Geneva Accords and Final Declaration included the following provisions:
- A ceasefire would take place between France and the Viet Minh.
- The 17th parallel would serve as a temporary dividing point between North and South Vietnam.
- The Viet Minh and its supporters would move north of the 17th parallel.
- The State of Vietnam would occupy the region south of the 17th parallel.
- Free elections would occur in January 1956.
- An international commission would supervise the elections.

The Geneva Accords was not a true peace agreement. Though the Final Declaration was intended to unify the country, it effectively split Vietnam into two nations: North Vietnam, a communist state supported by the Soviet Union and China; and South Vietnam, a noncommunist state aided and protected by the United States. Fearing the communists would win a popular election, the United States and South Vietnam never signed the Final Declaration. The elections never took place, and Vietnam remained divided for the next two decades.

DIEM AND NATION-STATE BUILDING (1955–1963)

US Support for Diem

In October 1955, Ngo Dinh Diem took control of South Vietnam. Born in 1933, Diem came from an aristocratic Roman Catholic family. He had rejected the opportunity to join Ho Chi Minh's insurgency against the French and spent most of the First Indochina War living in exile in Europe. After the Geneva Accords went into effect, Diem returned to South Vietnam. Diem initially agreed to serve as prime minister under Emperor Bao Dai. However, he swiftly set about consolidating his own political power. Diem used a government-controlled referendum to oust Bao Dai and declare himself president of the Republic of Vietnam. Diem made it clear that he was firmly opposed to communism. This won him strong backing from the United States. The United States wanted to see a stable government in South Vietnam, one which could withstand any incursions from the north.

Diem's Inadequacies

Once in power, Diem behaved more like a dictator than a president. He favored his own social class and Catholics over other groups, especially Vietnam's Buddhist majority. Diem took steps to repress any form of opposition, including outlawing religious and political groups that opposed his regime. Though he promised land reform, Diem's own connections to wealthy landowners made such progressive reforms impossible. A small elite retained control over South Vietnam's economy and politics, while guerilla groups sprang up in the countryside. The Diem government soon became mired in factionalism and disputes.

Violent protests disrupted Diem's efforts to create stability. Some of those protests occurred in the city of Saigon, the seat of Diem's power. Diem became increasingly dependent on US military aid to prop up his government.

US Military and Economic Assistance

The United States provided Diem with both military and financial aid. Though the financial aid was intended to help uplift the local economy, Diem used it mostly to reward his supporters. The larger population of South Vietnam saw little benefit from that aid. In addition, the United States helped Diem create an intelligence network that could identify and eliminate any communist sympathizers. This was part of a program known as **psychological warfare**, which aimed to win support for Diem and the United States, and deter communism without using violence. This later led to the slogan "winning hearts and minds." Unfortunately, violent conflict dominated the growing struggle in South Vietnam. During the First Indochina War, the United States had sent US soldiers to act as advisors. The United States continued to send these military advisors after the Geneva Accords. On July 8, 1959, two US soldiers died in an attack on a US compound 20 miles outside of Saigon. They are considered the first US war casualties in Vietnam.

The Growing Southern Insurgency

The anti-Diem insurgency in South Vietnam coalesced into a guerilla force called the **National Liberation Front**, or more popularly, the **Viet Cong**. North Vietnam sought to take advantage of Diem's difficulties and began to arm and train these guerilla forces. While not all opponents of the Diem regime were communists, the Viet Cong were both procommunist and pro-North Vietnam. With the rise of the Viet Cong, the conflict in the south became one between communism and anticommunism. Some members of Viet Cong units were former Viet Minh fighters who had remained in the south after the Geneva Accords. Others came from local peasant populations. Farmers felt betrayed by Diem's failed land reform and many believed communism promised better economic opportunities.

In 1959, the North Vietnamese forged a route through Laos and Cambodia that enabled them to supply the Viet Cong. This route became known as the Ho Chi Minh Trail. The trail was essential to North Vietnam's offensive in the south, so it was continually rebuilt and reinforced, even after many assaults from South Vietnamese and US forces. The exact relationship between the Viet Cong and the North Vietnamese Army was never precisely clear. The North Vietnamese claimed the Viet Cong was a largely indigenous movement led by South Vietnamese rebels. The United States believed that the Viet Cong was under the command of the North Vietnamese Army. Historians generally agree that by 1960, the Viet Cong was essentially an arm of the North Vietnamese Army (NVA).

The Viet Cong also regarded itself as a political party. In 1960, Viet Cong forces seized control of the province of Ben Trein in the Mekong Delta region. There, they set up a model communist government. Private property was abolished. Some residents found this government little better than Diem's authoritarian regime. The Viet Cong could be brutal toward anyone who resisted their rule. The choice between communism and a nationalist dictatorship was stark. People had to accept one or the other. Protesters who professed to be prodemocracy, anti-Diem, and anticommunist were increasingly marginalized in the conflict.

JFK's Commitment to Counterinsurgency

In 1960, American voters elected John Fitzgerald Kennedy president of the United States. Kennedy presented himself as a staunch "Cold Warrior." He was committed to containing communism and adhered to Eisenhower's domino theory. Kennedy offered Diem his support in preventing the spread of communism in South Vietnam. In May 1961, Kennedy sent a fleet of military helicopters and approximately 400 Special Forces soldiers, known as **Green Berets**, to South Vietnam to help Diem suppress the Viet Cong. The Green Berets are an elite, highly-trained cadre of the US Army that specializes in secret, or covert, operations. Kennedy's efforts were part of the anticommunist counterinsurgency. The term counterinsurgency implies that US forces were aiding South Vietnam in its fight against the Viet Cong. The United States was not yet officially in direct conflict with the North Vietnamese Army.

By the end of 1961, Kennedy had increased the number of US troops in South Vietnam to more than 16,000. In 1962, American aircraft began spraying the South Vietnamese countryside with **Agent Orange**, a powerful herbicide that could destroy large areas of vegetation. The US used Agent Orange to expose Viet Cong positions and render it impossible for insurgents to hide beneath the jungle canopy. Agent Orange contained powerful poisons that affected animals and humans as well as plants. The herbicide is linked to illness, birth defects, and even death. Well into the 1980s and 1990s, long after the Second Indochinese War was over, Agent Orange continued to affect American veterans and the Vietnamese people.

Internal Opposition Including the Buddhist Crisis

Many South Vietnamese regarded Diem's government as hopelessly corrupt. Diem had appointed family members who had little public-service experience to high government positions. Government offices and programs did not function. Officials on all levels of government solicited bribes. Diem used anticommunism to suppress any form of dissent, labeling his opponents communist sympathizers regardless of their politics. He favored Roman Catholics over other religions. This preference became a particularly bitter point with Diem's critics. Most Vietnamese were Buddhist. In May 1963, a group of Buddhists staged a peaceful protest in the city of Hue. South Vietnamese soldiers fired on the protestors, killing eight people. This event was the first in a series of protests called the **Buddhist Crisis**.

Buddhist monks enjoyed great respect in South Vietnam. The Vietnamese people saw them as educated and holy individuals. Buddhists looked to monks for leadership, and the monks set an example for others. In the summer of 1963, several anti-Diem Buddhist monks committed suicide by self-immolation. All around Saigon, they set fire to themselves in public places where they would draw attention and photographers. Their fiery protests attracted media attention worldwide. Diem faced growing international condemnation for his human rights abuses. Images of the burning monks came to symbolize the brutality and corruption in South Vietnam. Diem lost support even among his own military officers. Many Americans began to wonder why their nation should aid a dictator whose own people were ready to take their own lives rather than submit to his rule. The US government secretly conceded that Diem was a liability. Kennedy reportedly pressed Diem to resign from office but Diem refused.

The Coup Against Diem

On November 2, 1963, a group of South Vietnamese Army generals staged a coup, assassinating Diem and his brother Ngo Dinh Nhu. The CIA had helped plan the coup. The generals acted with the approval of the United States, though the level of US involvement remained secret at the time. According to some historians, the Americans did not want the generals to kill Diem. The United States merely wished Diem removed from power. Diem still commanded the loyalty of Vietnamese Catholics. If he became a martyr, the country would be further split. The generals tried to present Diem's death as a suicide, but the truth soon came out. South Vietnam entered a period of even greater turmoil.

Tran Le Xuan, known as Madame Nhu, was Nhu's wife and Diem's sister-in-law. She had been politically active and often visited the United States on behalf of Diem's government. After the coup, she fled to France where she became a fierce and outspoken critic of US policy in Vietnam. She frequently told reporters that the United States was directly responsible for the death of Diem and her husband. Madame Nhu said that all the "troubles" of the United States in Vietnam could be traced to the assassination of Diem. She lived in exile in France until her death in 2011.

LYNDON B. JOHNSON AMERICANIZES THE WAR (1964–1965)

Political Instability in Vietnam

The elimination of Diem failed to bring any stability to South Vietnam. The generals squabbled among themselves. Over the next two years, some 12 different military dictators attempted to rule the country. Each would-be ruler faced corruption and dissent. The Viet Cong used those weaknesses and the resulting confusion in South Vietnam to increase their attacks. Fearing South Vietnam might fall to communism, the US government felt it had no choice but to increase the American military presence.

Introduction of the North Vietnamese Army

Until the mid-1960s, North Vietnam had disrupted South Vietnam largely by supporting the Viet Cong. The North Vietnamese Army supplied weapons, equipment, and training, but did not send large units into South Vietnam itself. The assassination of Diem and the subsequent political upheaval convinced North Vietnamese leaders that South Vietnam was near collapse, and a surge in troops could bring them victory. North Vietnam staged a major offensive, moving troops into South Vietnam via the Ho Chi Minh Trail. By that time, the trail had become a major road. Truckloads of men and supplies entered South Vietnam via Laos and Cambodia. Both the Soviet Union and the People's Republic of China sent aid and military advisors to North Vietnam.

The Gulf of Tonkin Incident and Resolution

On November 22, 1963, President Kennedy was assassinated. His successor was his vice president, Lyndon B. Johnson. President Johnson was equally committed to the US effort in Vietnam; however, he knew that the presence of American troops in Vietnam had become a controversial political issue. By 1964, approximately 23,000 American troops were deployed in South Vietnam. Four hundred Americans had been killed.

Many Americans did not support increased US involvement in the region. Johnson's advisors believed that he should use air strikes against North Vietnam to stop the flow of troops and ammunition into South Vietnam. US air attacks on another country, however, might be construed as an act of war; the United States Congress had never formally declared war against North Vietnam. While Johnson was ready to use air power, he worried that he did not have the legal authority to order strikes directly against North Vietnam. He was concerned about public reaction if he sent in bombers without the consent of Congress.

In early August 1964, Johnson received news that two US Navy destroyers, the USS *Maddox* and the USS *Turner Joy*, had been attacked by North Vietnamese torpedo boats in the Gulf of Tonkin. Details of both attacks were obscure. The Gulf of Tonkin is located off the coast of North Vietnam on the South China Sea. The USS *Maddox* was probably there to collect intelligence. When North Vietnamese boats came too close, the commander of the *Maddox* felt threatened. He may have fired the first shots to warn them off. The North Vietnamese fired back, and a short skirmish ensued in which several North Vietnamese sailors died. There were no US casualties, nor did the *Maddox* suffer any serious damage. Two days later, the commander of the *Turner Joy* reported a torpedo attack. Subsequent research revealed that this attack may not have occurred. Nevertheless, the news of two US Navy ships coming under fire from enemy vessels gave Johnson the pretext he needed to ask Congress for the power to launch an offensive directly against North Vietnam.

On August 7, Congress passed the **Gulf of Tonkin Resolution**. This resolution declared that as commander in chief, the president has the power to do whatever he deems necessary to protect US military personnel in Southeast Asia from attack. Specifically, it said that the president could "take all necessary measures to repel any armed attack against the forces of the United States and to prevent further aggression." The president did not need to consult Congress or wait for a formal declaration of war in order to act. In addition, the resolution emphasized that peace and security in Southeast Asia was vital to American interests. The resolution passed in the House of Representatives by a vote of 414–0. Only two senators voted against it, making the Senate vote 88–2. The broad wording of the resolution granted the president almost unlimited power to increase the number of US troops in Vietnam and engage in air strikes against North Vietnam. The passage of the Gulf of Tonkin Resolution led directly to the escalation of the war. It also spurred the growing antiwar movement among the American people.

The Role of Vietnam in the 1964 Presidential Campaign

The war in Vietnam emerged as a campaign issue in the 1964 presidential election. Johnson, a Democrat, ran against Republican candidate Senator Barry Goldwater of Arizona. Some people had criticized Johnson for the Gulf of Tonkin Resolution. However, the media frequently portrayed

Goldwater as the more extreme "hawk." Goldwater had openly suggested that nuclear weapons might be an option in Vietnam. Even those Democrats who supported the war stopped short of advocating the use of atomic weapons like the H-bomb. Both the United States and the Soviet Union possessed nuclear warheads. If the United States used nuclear weapons on North Vietnam, the Soviet Union might conceivably defend their ally by deploying its own nuclear bombs on South Vietnam. Nuclear escalation could potentially lead to World War III and global annihilation. This scenario may seem unlikely in retrospect, but it felt very real to voters in 1964.

The Democratic Party capitalized on those fears by running television ads implying that Goldwater was an extremist who should not have his hand on the nuclear "button." The most famous of those ads showed an innocent little girl plucking petals one by one from a daisy. As she does so, a voice in the background begins a countdown followed by an image of a nuclear explosion. Viewers found the "Daisy" ad so disturbing that it only aired once. But the message it conveyed was so clear that historians credit the ad with propelling Johnson to a landslide victory. Johnson saw the victory as an endorsement of his own policies in Vietnam. Shortly after his inauguration in January 1965, he ordered a sustained bombing campaign that targeted North Vietnam.

US Air Campaign over Vietnam: Flaming Dart to Rolling Thunder

In February 1965, the United States initiated air strikes against North Vietnam. **Operation Flaming Dart** took place between February 7 and 24. The operation started when the US Air Force bombed a military base near the North Vietnamese port of Dong Hoi. At the same time, the South Vietnamese Air Force attacked enemy communications centers near the border dividing North and South Vietnam. On February 19, the US Air Force employed B-57 jet bombers to assist South Vietnamese forces in the Central Highlands. President Johnson announced to the American public that these strikes were retaliation for Viet Cong assaults on American bases in the city of Pleiku. However, their real importance and purpose was to intimidate North Vietnam into surrender. The United States possessed massive air power. The North Vietnamese had a small air force consisting mostly of planes supplied by the Soviet Union. Americans thought it impossible that North Vietnam could persevere under such sustained bombardment.

On March 2, 1965, **Operation Rolling Thunder** began with attacks on the southern border of North Vietnam. The US Air Force planned to start by attacking sites below the 19th parallel and gradually move the bombing northward. The United States hoped that the threat of bombardment would force North Vietnam to call for peace talks. The North Vietnamese government insisted that peace talks could only take place if the bombing stopped and the United States withdrew completely from South Vietnam. Johnson had no intention of withdrawing without victory. As the bombing continued, the North Vietnamese dug in and mounted a surprisingly effective resistance, using Soviet made anti-aircraft guns and surface-to-air missiles. These weapons did not stop the air raids, but they did bring many aircraft down.

In April, Rolling Thunder turned its attention to the supply routes that connected North Vietnam to China and the Soviet Union. Bombing raids targeted bridges, river ports, and communications centers. The North Vietnamese responded by rebuilding and repairing. The bombing did not seem to be bringing the end of the conflict any closer, so Johnson escalated the war once more by increasing air strikes.

More than 5,000 American servicemen were killed during the bombing campaigns. Most of the Americans the North Vietnamese took prisoner were pilots or other airmen. For years on end, they remained in North Vietnamese prisons under harsh and brutal conditions. All told, the United States dropped an estimated seven million tons of bombs on North Vietnam, Laos, and Cambodia during the war. This total is greater than the total bombs dropped by the allies on Europe and Asia during World War II. Not all bombs exploded upon impact. Unexploded bombs, or **ordinance**, have remained a danger to civilians into the twenty-first century.

Introduction of US Combat Troops (March through April 1965)

In March 1965, Johnson further escalated US involvement by dispatching 3,500 Marines to South Vietnam. The Marines were the first American ground troops to engage in combat operations in Vietnam. Previously, servicemen only advised and supported the South Vietnamese Army. The South Vietnamese Army proved chronically weak and seemed unlikely to defeat the North Vietnamese even with US aid. However, these new troops would engage directly with the North Vietnamese Army and the Viet Cong. The Marines landed in the port city of Da Nang in central Vietnam. The original plan was to use ground troops defensively, only engaging the enemy when they were attacked. Unfortunately, it soon became clear that if they were to survive in Vietnam, US troops would need to employ both defensive and offensive tactics.

Increase in US Combat Commitment (July 1965)

By June, the number of US military deployed to South Vietnam had increased to around 8,200. In July, Johnson signed an order calling for the deployment of an additional 100,000 troops to Vietnam. Many Americans supported the deployment of ground troops because they thought this push would hasten the end of the conflict. Others objected to Johnson's actions, claiming he was abusing the powers granted to him by the Gulf of Tonkin Resolution. Johnson was aware of his critics, but he persisted in his policy of escalation. He hoped that the fresh troops could turn the tide of the war and save South Vietnam from communism.

AMERICA TAKES CHARGE (1965–1967)

Westmoreland's Strategy of Attrition

In 1964, General William Westmoreland took command of US forces in Vietnam. Westmoreland believed that the United States would have to take the offensive for the US to win the war in Vietnam. He had little faith in the abilities of the South Vietnamese Army to defeat the enemy. He insisted that US forces should take the initiative in military operations. Under his leadership, the role of South Vietnam decreased and the responsibilities of the United States grew.

Westmoreland's main goal was to defeat North Vietnam through **attrition warfare**, a military strategy consisting of a series of relentless attacks from both ground and air designed to wear the enemy down. These assaults were meant to cripple the Viet Cong and drive the North Vietnamese out of South Vietnam. Rather than focusing on seizing and controlling territory, Westmoreland argued that US soldiers should simply kill as many enemy combatants as they possibly could.

Westmoreland needed a substantial ground force to carry out his strategy. He did not want a limit placed on the number of soldiers he could request. If his demands for fresh troops were met, he assured Johnson that the United States could declare victory by 1967. The United States, not South Vietnam, now carried the major burden of the war.

Measures of Success

Because the United States did not intend to invade and occupy North Vietnam, measuring success on the battlefield proved difficult. Military campaigns traditionally show their progress on maps that clearly define territory won and lost. But no such map existed during the war in Vietnam. American troops might engage the enemy in a certain valley or hamlet only to withdraw to their own base to later re-engage the enemy in the same place. American soldiers might sweep through an area several times to seek out Viet Cong and North Vietnamese troops. To measure success of the American offensive, Westmoreland relied on the body count. After each clash, American commanders would report the number of enemy combatants killed. A high number meant a high degree of success.

Several problems weakened this system. First, commanders might exaggerate the body count in order to please their superiors and make their troops look good. Second, many Viet Cong did not wear uniforms, so dead civilians could easily be included in the body count even if they did not actually fight. Third, neither the Viet Cong nor the North Vietnamese had the resources to remove their dead from the field. The same body might be counted twice or even three times. The high body counts touted by Westmoreland as proof of battlefield success were later revealed to be grossly exaggerated.

The Continuing Air War

The air war continued over North Vietnam. The United States began to target major cities like the capital city of Hanoi and the port city of Haiphong. The North Vietnamese government evacuated its urban populations to the countryside. Many people retreated into caves or lived underground. North Vietnam's leaders insisted that morale remained high, and the bombing only strengthened their people's resolve. Given that the government was a dictatorship, it is clear the North Vietnamese people had little choice but to continue their resistance, despite large civilian casualties. Their true feelings remained hidden.

An additional air operation, known as **Steel Tiger**, focused on bombing the Ho Chi Minh Trail in an effort to disrupt the flow of men and supplies traveling through Laos into South Vietnam. As before, North Vietnam responded by mobilizing its people to repair and rebuild.

The bombing campaigns contributed to the rising antiwar sentiment in the United States. People began to criticize the air war as expensive and ineffective. News photos of dead civilians outraged the American public.

The Impact of the War on Vietnamese Society

The war intensified social divisions and tensions in Vietnam, particularly in the south. Although the repeated bombings devastated much of North Vietnam, most of the land battles took place in South Vietnam. Large sections of the countryside were destroyed. Peasant farmers found themselves torn between the Viet Cong and American forces. The Viet Cong would confiscate rice and livestock and conscript villagers into building tunnels and transporting supplies. Anyone suspected of collaborating with the Americans could be tortured or executed. Americans posed their own threats. Unable to distinguish between ordinary civilians and Viet Cong, US soldiers might shoot and kill indiscriminately. Women and children were as suspect in the eyes of Americans as Vietnamese men, for they could carry messages for the Viet Cong or even hide grenades and weapons. Rural people felt persecuted by both sides. Hunger and privation marked their lives.

Some South Vietnamese profited from the war. The surge in American troops brought an influx of consumer goods. The military PX or Post Exchange near Saigon was one of the largest stores in the world, selling everything from cigarettes and cameras to American blue jeans. In Saigon, a thriving black market developed that resold items from the PX to Vietnamese civilians. Other South Vietnamese found more legitimate jobs working as translators and guides for American journalists. The American embassy also employed Vietnamese locals as clerical workers and phone operators. Income from these jobs helped workers rise into the middle class.

Soldiers introduced American popular culture to South Vietnam. Young South Vietnamese became familiar with American music, movies, and slang. There was also a darker side to the American-fueled economy. Street drugs such as heroin and opium proliferated. Bars often promoted prostitution. Unmarried Vietnamese women who had children by American men were often shunned and ostracized by their communities. Government corruption made economic stability difficult for most people. Even those who gained a foothold in the middle class faced uncertainty. Class divisions between rich and poor still determined how most people lived and worked.

Stabilization of the Saigon Regime

In 1965, the South Vietnamese government achieved some degree of stability when General Nguyen Cao Ky and General Nguyen Van Thieu seized power. They were supposed to rule jointly with Thieu as a kind of figurehead president while Ky served as a military prime minister controlling the government behind the scenes. Their joint government lasted two years and broke the cycle of coups that had brought a new regime at least once a year. Ky and Thieu, more rivals than colleagues, shared an uneasy relationship. Thieu undermined Ky's power and placed his own supporters in government positions. In 1971, he staged a rigged election that made him sole ruler. Thieu remained in power until the US withdrawal in 1975. Thieu's government was often accused of corruption, and like his many predecessors, he suppressed dissent with force. Though he called himself a president, Thieu was a dictator. South Vietnam never became a true democracy.

America's Army in Vietnam

When they arrived in the country, most American soldiers were totally unfamiliar with Vietnamese culture and language. Many of the soldiers were still in their late teens and had never left home before. Vietnam was a new, alien, and potentially deadly world. Lack of cultural preparation often led to a sense of suspicion and hostility toward the Vietnamese on the part of these young Americans. Most soldiers deployed to Vietnam for short periods of one year. This policy meant that the United States always had fresh troops, but it also made it difficult for soldiers to learn more about Vietnam and its people, even when they wanted to. Short deployments also disrupted military tactics as soldiers were focused on going home rather than winning the war. Ordinary enlisted men had little chance to form bonds with officers, and officers had little opportunity to gain leadership experience. Career officers could return for additional deployments, but they would find themselves leading yet another group of new men. It seemed the endless supply of new soldiers and officers ensured that the government could prolong the war for years. Despite these challenges, some soldiers did form close bonds, and some developed friendships with Vietnamese people.

Between 1964 and 1973, three million American soldiers served in Vietnam. About 47,000 of these soldiers were killed in combat. Another 10,000 died in accidents or by other means. Slightly more than 150,000 were wounded. Two-thirds of those who served were volunteers. The others had been drafted. The average age of American servicemen was 23.

War without Fronts: The Combat Experience

Unlike other wars, the war in Vietnam had no front lines. Combat could take place almost anywhere. Most battles occurred in jungle terrain, called **in-country** by American soldiers. Physical conditions were arduous. The climate was hot and humid. During the monsoon season, soldiers endured torrential rains. The mud and dampness led to fungal infections and foot problems. Tropical diseases like malaria spread easily. Soldiers had to carry their own food and fresh water. Pathways were dense with tangled overgrowth. Often, the only way in or out of an area was by helicopter or on foot. Soldiers walked patrols in single file. The lead soldier was said to be "walking point," the most dangerous position. The man up front would be the first to encounter landmines or sniper fire.

American soldiers faced a dedicated enemy who had years of experience in jungle combat and knew how to blend into the environment. Viet Cong and North Vietnamese guerilla fighters were experts in setting landmines and booby traps. Any dead body might be wired with explosives to kill anyone who came near. Americans did have certain advantages over their enemy. The average American soldier was healthier and very well fed. Americans had superior weapons and their sick and wounded received better medical care. American soldiers also became adept at guerilla warfare. They learned how to set traps, move silently, and detect hidden tunnels. Even critics of the war agreed that American troops fought bravely and well. The problems lay not with ordinary soldiers but with their political leadership.

Search and Destroy: Ia Drang Valley

General Westmoreland instituted a military strategy known as **search and destroy**, which depended on a swift attack and withdrawal. US soldiers would deploy into an area, at times dropped by helicopter. Their mission was to locate the enemy, kill them, then withdraw before their presence attracted reinforcements. Search and destroy was part of Westmoreland's overall policy of aiming for maximum enemy kills rather than taking territory and defending it.

On November 14–16, 1965, US troops in the central highlands of South Vietnam met the North Vietnamese Army at Ia Drang Valley. Ia Drang marked the first major encounter between US and North Vietnamese forces. It was also the first time the US military used large numbers of helicopters in combat. The helicopters inserted soldiers into the valley, dropped supplies, provided air support, rescued wounded soldiers, and removed the survivors when the battle was over.

The **Battle of Ia Drang** began when an American battalion dropped into the valley for a search and destroy mission. Their commander had been told a North Vietnamese battalion was in the area. However, there were actually three battalions of NVA soldiers. Over a three-day period, Americans amassed approximately 1,000 soldiers at the battle site. The North Vietnamese force was a little more than twice that number. Though heavily outnumbered, the American forces managed to inflict significant casualties on the enemy. In the end, the US forces lost around 250 soldiers with an additional 245 wounded. The North Vietnamese forces lost approximately 1,200 soldiers with some 500 wounded.

Though the battle was more of a stalemate, each side claimed victory. Neither side accomplished anything decisive; still, each learned something about the other. The North Vietnamese got a preview of American helicopter power. They realized they could neutralize air attacks by getting as close as possible to the American forces. Helicopter pilots would not fire if they feared hitting their own soldiers. The US Army acknowledged that the North Vietnamese Army was far more disciplined and determined than previously thought. General Westmoreland still believed his war of attrition would lead to victory. However, the US government knew by now that this war could not be won by 1967.

HOME FRONT USA (1963–1967)

The Great Society: Guns vs. Butter

After Lyndon B. Johnson was elected president in 1964, he rolled out a program of civil rights initiatives and social reforms he called the **Great Society**. He believed his landslide victory had given him a mandate to enact sweeping changes in domestic policy as well in foreign affairs. Between 1964 and 1965, Congress approved funds for healthcare, education, job training, public works, and urban renewal.

One of the centerpieces of the Great Society was a group of programs that came to be known as the **War on Poverty**. These programs included the Food Stamp Act, Head Start, the Job Corps, the Economic Opportunity Act, the Higher Education Act, and Volunteers in Service to America (VISTA). Johnson also sponsored bills to establish Medicaid, Medicare, the Public Broadcasting System, and the National Highway Traffic Safety Administration. All these ambitious changes came at a price; under Johnson's administration, spending on education and healthcare alone tripled.

At the same time he was trying to eliminate poverty at home, President Johnson was also escalating the US commitment in Vietnam. Both his critics and his supporters warned that he wanted to provide both "guns and butter." He wanted domestic reforms, but he would not abandon the war. While President Johnson tried to balance the monetary needs of his war on poverty and the war in Vietnam, he inevitably had to siphon money from social programs to support the war.

The controversy over Vietnam dominated President Johnson's years in office. His support among progressives eroded as the war escalated. Today, Johnson is recognized for his many reforms but he is also remembered as a president whose achievements were overshadowed by his commitment to a failed war.

The Credibility Gap

During the 1960s, the term **credibility gap** was used to describe the difference between how Johnson and his officials presented events in Vietnam and the reality of the war. Johnson wished to convince the American public that the United States was winning. However, reports from journalists and statements from returning soldiers suggested something quite different, that the United States had become mired in an unwinnable war. Senator William J. Fulbright of Arkansas referred to a credibility gap when he felt that Johnson failed to give an honest answer about the war. Some historians credit Fulbright with coining the term, though it may have appeared in the press earlier.

When people talked about Johnson's credibility gap, they often cited Westmoreland's body counts. The body counts reported by the military were far too high to be realistic. The American public began to wonder who and what was right. If they could not believe the most basic things their government said about the war in Vietnam, how could they believe anything it said at all?

Congressional Dissent

President Johnson's critics in Congress included both Democrats and Republicans. Not all members of Johnson's own party supported his policies in Vietnam. In 1964, Congress had voted almost unanimously to pass the Gulf of Tonkin Resolution. By 1966, public pressure from the growing antiwar movement forced many members of Congress to reconsider their support for the war. In February 1966, the Senate Foreign Relations Committee held a series of public hearings on Vietnam, led by Senator Fulbright, a Democrat. Often called the **Fulbright Hearings**, the televised hearings became a national event. Senators openly questioned Johnson's decision to continue bombing North Vietnam and his request for more troops in South Vietnam. The overall intention of the hearings was to demonstrate that Johnson's administration had failed to be honest with Americans. Furious at what he perceived to be disloyalty, Johnson did his best to ignore the committee and continued with his policy of escalating the war.

The committee heard testimony from other members of Congress, former servicemen, and members of the public. Among those who testified were John Kerry, a former naval officer and head of the nonprofit organization Vietnam Veterans Against the War. In his 1971 statement to the committee, he asked how the government could "ask a man to be the last man to die for a mistake?"

The committee continued to meet until 1971. While it failed to stop the war entirely, it was one of the many factors that eventually pushed the government to de-escalate the war. In 1975, the United States finally withdrew from Vietnam.

Television and the Press

Vietnam is sometimes called America's first televised war. For the first time in history, people could see moving images of war right in their own living rooms. Film footage from Vietnam appeared regularly on the nightly news. Through television, all Americans began to feel connected to the war in a way that was not previously possible. It should be noted that satellite technology was still very limited and the film footage was not transmitted live from Vietnam. Film footage was usually edited in press offices in Tokyo, Japan, and then flown to the United States. Nevertheless, images and interviews with young soldiers made an enormous impact on how Americans felt about the war.

Print journalists and photographers also influenced public perceptions. On June 8, 1972, Nick Ut, a photographer for the Associated Press, snapped a photo of a group of children fleeing a napalm attack by the South

Vietnamese Army. One girl's back was on fire. The image appeared on the front pages of newspapers nationwide. Ut's photograph became one of the most iconic images of the war, symbolizing everything that seemed to be wrong with Vietnam.

Not all journalists opposed the war. The military had its own newspaper, *Stars and Stripes,* which regularly issued positive stories about American servicemen and the progress of the war. Many civilian news outlets supported the war. Some historians believe that the press did not become explicitly "antiwar" until the late 1960s. One major turning point came during anchorman Walter Cronkite's nightly news broadcast for CBS. Cronkite was one of America's most popular and admired journalists. He had been a reporter during World War II and was considered more conservative and patriotic than other major news anchors. In February 1968, he remarked that the United States seemed to be "mired in stalemate" in Vietnam. Cronkite's brief statement was taken as a sign that the average American had finally turned against the war. Even President Johnson admitted to his aides, "If I've lost Cronkite, I've lost Middle America."

The Civil Rights Movement

Johnson's **Civil Rights Act of 1964** is considered the most far-reaching civil rights legislation since the Civil War. Signed into law on July 2, 1964, the Civil Rights Act signaled the federal government's commitment to end racial segregation and discrimination. Johnson considered the promotion of civil rights essential to his domestic platform. The war in Vietnam, however, placed him at odds with many civil rights leaders and cost him the support of many African American and Hispanic voters.

African American and Hispanic soldiers served in disproportionate numbers in Vietnam. Many came from poor families and could not receive college exemptions from the draft. Some joined the service because they lived in areas of high unemployment and felt they had no other job opportunities. While African Americans represented around 11–12 percent of the total population during the war, 22 percent of the 58,000 servicemen killed in Vietnam were African American. Statistics regarding Hispanic soldiers are more difficult to verify, as many of those soldiers were listed as white. According to a 2018 opinion piece in the *New York Times*, Hispanics represented about 12 percent of the population in the 1960s and early 1970s but made up about 19 percent of all military casualties in Vietnam.

The high numbers of African American and Hispanic soldiers serving in Vietnam caused families to feel that the burden of war fell disproportionately on minority communities. Many antiwar activists claimed that Vietnam was a war fought by poor African American soldiers for a government that consisted mostly of rich, white men. However, there were more white men serving as soldiers than minorities. Regardless, the public's perception reveals that by the late 1960s, the war had become less about containing communism and more about a government that sacrificed soldiers because it could not admit its mistakes.

Returning African American and Hispanic soldiers faced racism and job discrimination. Civil rights leader Martin Luther King Jr. openly criticized the war. As an advocate of nonviolence, King had always been officially antiwar, but during the early 1960s, he put his civil rights work first. By 1967, Dr. King led an antiwar march in Chicago, making it clear that he no longer saw a gap between support for civil rights and opposition to the war. On April 4, 1967, he told a crowd that the government was sending black soldiers to Vietnam to fight for freedom in Asia that they did not have in the United States.

Many African American and Hispanic soldiers considered themselves patriots. They were proud of their service and the sacrifices they made. However, support for Johnson and the war continued to decline among African Americans and Hispanics as the election of 1968 drew near.

The Genesis of the New Left

In the United States, the term **left** can refer to a wide range of political positions. Left can apply to anyone from radical anarchists, who believe in no government at all, to traditional liberals, who support individual rights and freedoms under limited government. After World War II, the mainstream American left was generally pro-democracy and antidictatorships. The Cold War made liberals anticommunists. Leftists originally supported the war in Vietnam because they saw South Vietnam as a democracy fighting the North Vietnamese communist dictatorship. This was the position taken by President Kennedy and later by President Johnson. Liberals also tended to support civil rights and social reforms, a modification of the classic liberal belief in small government.

The antiwar movement that emerged in the late 1960s characterized itself as more anti-imperialist than anticommunist. Anti-imperialism was an objection to the idea that rich and powerful states should have the power to impose their will on smaller, less developed states. Antiwar activists both at home and abroad accused the United States of attempting to colonize South Vietnam. They saw US military actions in Vietnam as a kind of "empire building," a desire on the part of the United States to expand its influence and power in the region at the expense of the local people. The United States, in their eyes, was not helping the South Vietnamese fend off a communist dictatorship. Rather, it was viewed as usurping the right of the Vietnamese people to control their own country.

A more radicalized **New Left** emerged from the antiwar movement. These activists expanded their criticism of the war to include a critique of American society as a whole. Some of them saw capitalism as the root of social problems. They advocated for a system that would redistribute wealth and even eliminate private property. More extreme factions of the left, such as the Weather Underground, declared that the US government itself should be overthrown and replaced. Critics of the antiwar movement accused the new left of being anti-American and procommunist. Public demonstrations against the war often turned violent. Americans on all sides of the debate began to fear that the conflict over the war in Vietnam would tear the country apart.

The Draft and Draft Resistance

When the United States committed combat troops to the war in Vietnam in 1965, all male citizens age 18 and older were subject to the **draft**. Being drafted meant being conscripted into the military. The Selective Service oversaw the draft. Technically, the draft applied to all men between the ages of 18 and 45. Men were required to register with their local branch of the Selective Service upon their eighteenth birthday or when they became naturalized citizens if they were adults under 45.

Men could be exempted from the draft for various reasons. Physical limitations and disabilities could prevent a man from serving. Married men with children could also be exempted. Conscientious objectors who opposed war for religious or moral reasons could be freed from the obligation to serve, though not all requested exemption. Some conscientious objectors felt they could serve in the military as long as they were not directly involved in combat. Men enrolled in college could request a deferment. Deferment did not exempt them from the draft entirely. They could still be drafted after graduation. As the war in Vietnam became more unpopular, thousands of young American men enrolled in college to avoid service in Vietnam. Because most college students tend to be middle class, the draft began to draw largely on men who came from lower income families.

Colleges became centers of antiwar activity and draft-resistance. In 1964, young men started to publicly burn their draft cards from the Selective Service to dramatize their objections to the war. These events drew the attention of press and the idea of draft-resistance spread. Some of those who could not gain exemption fled to Canada and other foreign countries to avoid the draft. The US government considered them fugitives from the law. In 1967, black athlete and boxing champion Muhammad Ali was sentenced to five years in prison for refusing to be drafted. He did not go to jail and his conviction was overturned four years later. However, his willingness to risk jail rather than fight in Vietnam made him a popular hero to the antiwar movement.

By 1970, the number of men seeking draft exemptions outnumbered draftees. In 1971, President Richard Nixon abolished the draft in favor of a lottery system that would choose candidates at random based on their birthdates. The draft lottery was even less popular than the draft and generated more protests. In 1973, the US government officially ended the draft and the US Army began to rely entirely on volunteers.

TET (1968)

Vietnamese Planning for the Tet Offensive

The US air strikes and ground offensive took a tremendous toll on the North Vietnamese military and civilians alike. To a certain extent, Westmoreland's war of attrition had worked. While North Vietnamese government officials publicly declared that the North Vietnamese people stood firm against the United States, in reality morale was low. The North Vietnamese government needed to mount its own major offensive to unite the country and prove that the war was winnable. In addition, North Vietnam's leadership was in crisis. The aging Ho Chi Minh was seriously ill and close to death. Although the North Vietnamese still revered Ho as the leader of their country, his actual role in the government had declined. Several factions within the government vied for power. A successful offensive could bring those factions together and prevent the government from collapsing.

In 1967, General Vo Nguyen Giap, the head of North Vietnamese defense, began planning an action called the **General Offensive and Uprising**. This military operation became known as the **Tet Offensive**, because it was scheduled to start on a holiday called Tet. Tet was the first day of the Vietnamese Lunar New Year. In 1968, Tet fell on January 31. In both North and South Vietnam, families and friends gathered to celebrate the holiday, which had usually been observed with a ceasefire. The North Vietnamese decided to take advantage of the annual "day of peace" because no one would expect an attack on Tet. In coordination with the Viet Cong, the North Vietnamese Army would launch a series of more than 100 separate assaults throughout South Vietnam. They even planned to attack the US embassy in Saigon.

In the days before the offensive, the North Vietnamese Army transported men and supplies into South Vietnam via the Ho Chi Minh Trail. The exact number of combined Viet Cong and North Vietnamese Army troops involved in the Tet Offensive is not known. The total force was estimated between 85,000 and may have been as high as 200,000.

On January 21, ten days before the Tet Offensive, a force of North Vietnamese and Viet Cong attacked the US base in Khe Sanh, a city on the northwest border of South Vietnam. North Vietnam staged the battle as a diversionary tactic. The fighting was fierce. The North Vietnamese hoped that while the American military was focused on Khe Sanh, it would fail to notice increased activity along the Ho Chi Minh Trail. The US Army later disputed reports that its troops had been distracted by the firefight in Khe Sanh, but historians note that the use of the battle as a diversion by the North Vietnamese did have some effect on delaying the American response to Tet.

Communist Objectives

The objectives in the Tet Offensive were political and psychological as well as military. The North Vietnamese knew that the government of South Vietnam was weak and unstable. The communists hoped the offensive would spark an uprising among the people. When the South Vietnamese realized that neither their own government nor the Americans could protect them, they would have no choice but to side with North Vietnam.

North Vietnam was also aware that support for the war was waning among Americans. The communists believed that the force of their attack, especially in Saigon, would demoralize the US military and the American public. If the communists could attack the US embassy, American soldiers would fear there was no safe place in Vietnam. More US casualties would further weaken the American support for the war.

Above all, the communist objective was to convince both the people of South Vietnam and the United States that they could not win the war against such a determined and disciplined enemy force.

The Tet Offensive

The Tet Offensive began in the early hours of January 31, 1968 and lasted three days. Communist troops attacked at least 120 targets in South Vietnam, including five major cities, many regional capitals, and dozens of rural hamlets. Overall, the North Vietnamese attacks were not very successful. The sheer number of battle sites spread their forces thin, making it difficult to hold the positions they had seized. Once the South Vietnamese and US forces rallied, they drove off most of the invaders. However, the North Vietnamese attack on Saigon did score a psychological victory. News images of combat taking place in the very courtyard of the US embassy rattled American citizens as well as the international community. Although the embassy later was secured from a takeover, Americans received the lasting impression of US vulnerability in the face of North Vietnamese aggression.

One of the major sites of the Tet Offensive was the city of Hue, located about 50 miles south of the 17th parallel that divided the two Vietnams. Hue was a large and historic city known for its ancient temples and palaces. Communist troops stormed into Hue and proceeded to round up and execute anyone believed to be associated with the Americans or the South Vietnamese government. The massacre claimed the lives of more than 5,000 civilian residents of the city.

The **Battle of Hue** lasted three weeks. It was one of the longest battles of the war. Much of the city was reduced to rubble. On February 26, American and South Vietnamese forces recaptured Hue. The 5,000 North Vietnamese troops killed during the Tet Offensive far outnumbered the casualties suffered by the Americans and South Vietnamese forces. The United States lost 150 Marines and approximately 400 South Vietnamese soldiers died.

Reactions in the United States and Saigon

The Tet Offensive was not a defeat for US forces in Vietnam. Still, the violent assault was a public relations disaster for the United States. The North Vietnamese had succeeded in demoralizing the Americans. However, the communist plan failed to trigger a mass rebellion among the South Vietnamese. Though South Vietnam's government remained weak, reports of the massacre at Hue made many people turn against North Vietnam. In the wake of the Tet Offensive, General Westmoreland asked President Johnson to send 200,000 fresh troops to South Vietnam.

President Johnson was becoming worn down by the antiwar protests that raged throughout America. It was clear that American citizens wanted the war to end. So Johnson turned down Westmoreland's request for reinforcements, refusing to commit more American troops to the conflict. President Johnson decided instead to scale back US military operations in Vietnam. He started by limiting US bombing runs to a narrow region of North Vietnam below the 20th parallel.

LBJ Decides Not to Run

On March 31, Lyndon Johnson held a press conference to announce he would refuse the Democratic nomination in 1968. His statement shocked the nation as most voters had assumed President Johnson would win re-election. Many people viewed his decision as an admission that the controversy over the Vietnam War destroyed his chances to win another term. President Johnson spent the rest of his remaining months in office working to arrange peace talks to end the war. However, it would take seven more years before the conflict in Vietnam would end.

Bombing Halt and Beginning of Peace Talks

Concurrent with his decision not to seek re-election, Johnson declared that he would halt bombing if North Vietnam agreed to peace negotiations. In May 1968, representatives of the United States, North Vietnam, South Vietnam, and the Provisional Revolutionary Government of South Vietnam (also known as the Viet Cong) met in Paris to discuss an end to the war. The United States wanted the Viet Cong to cease all military activities before agreeing to a complete halt in bombing. But progress proved to be slow. Johnson had hoped to broker a lasting peace in Vietnam before he left office, but his chances of making that a reality were slipping away. In America, public pressure to stop the bombing continued to build. On October 31,

1968, President Johnson announced that the United States would cease all bombing if North Vietnam continued to negotiate in Paris. The bombing stopped on November 1. The cessation represented the end of Operation Rolling Thunder, which had begun three years earlier.

The Election of 1968

President Johnson's decision not run for president left the Democratic nomination wide open. Most Democratic voters opposed the war and had hopes their party would field a "peace" candidate. Minnesota senator Eugene McCarthy had openly declared his opposition to the war. Back on March 12, McCarthy had finished second in the New Hampshire primary, just behind Johnson. McCarthy's strong showing was one of the factors that prompted Johnson's announcement three weeks later.

On March 16, Massachusetts senator Robert F. Kennedy, a former US attorney general and brother of President John F. Kennedy, had also entered the presidential race. Kennedy was a charismatic figure known for his work promoting civil rights and fighting poverty. Many of his supporters were antiwar activists and progressives. Kennedy was especially popular among younger voters. On June 5, 1968, Kennedy won the California primary. He gave a victory speech in a Los Angeles hotel ballroom as his supporters cheered. But moments later, the senator was mortally wounded by an assassin's bullet. The nation reeled. Kennedy's murder came just two months after the assassination of civil rights leader Martin Luther King, Jr. The two shocking tragedies made people fear that American society itself was on the verge of collapse. For members of the peace movement, Robert Kennedy's death dashed their hopes of success in the 1968 election.

President Johnson's vice president, Hubert H. Humphrey, became the frontrunner for the Democratic nomination. But antiwar activists resented Humphrey for having supported Johnson's war policies. They did not care that Johnson also urged the peace talks and halted the bombing in Vietnam. President Johnson's long struggle with the war had stained the reputation of his vice president. Humphrey's nomination would split the Democratic Party apart.

Richard M. Nixon became the Republican candidate. Nixon, Dwight Eisenhower's vice president, had run against John F. Kennedy in 1960 and lost. Richard Nixon won the election of 1968. The popular vote was extremely close, giving Nixon a margin of slightly more than 500,000 votes. However, the Electoral College gave Nixon a solid plurality of votes—301 to

Humphrey's 191. George Wallace, a third-party candidate, received 46 electoral votes.

Nixon's election in 1968 was not without controversy, though. Many people accused Nixon of undermining the Paris Peace Talks in order to sabotage Humphrey's chances. As president, Nixon inherited the Vietnam War. Like Johnson before him, Nixon would find it difficult to end what was proving to be America's longest war.

VIETNAMIZING THE WAR (1969–1973)

Nixon, Kissinger, and Vietnamization

After taking office in 1969, Richard Nixon began a process of shifting the burden of the war to the South Vietnamese Army and government, a process he called **Vietnamization**. Under Vietnamization, the United States would be responsible for giving the South Vietnamese Army additional training and weapons in order to prepare them for an eventual US troop withdrawal. In addition, the United States would give South Vietnam substantial economic support. Concurrent with the troop withdrawals, Nixon also started bombing raids along the Laotian and Cambodian borders to stop North Vietnam from using those countries as entry points to South Vietnam.

President Nixon relied on the leadership of his National Security Advisor Henry Kissinger. Kissinger had come to the United States in 1938 as a German-Jewish refugee. He served in the US Army during World War II and later attended Harvard University where he received a doctorate in political science. Kissinger promoted a theory called **realpolitik**, a government policy based on practical considerations, not ideology. He placed a high value on diplomacy and negotiation. Kissinger was anticommunist, but he also believed that the United States could establish peaceful relationships with the Soviet Union and the People's Republic of China. This lowering of Cold War tensions between the United States and the communist bloc countries was known as **detente**. Kissinger saw the continued US involvement in Vietnam as an impediment to detente. The United States didn't have to use military force to contain communism. It could use diplomacy.

Justifications for Vietnamization (Troop Withdrawal)

Kissinger wanted the United States to withdraw from Vietnam, but he feared that if Americans simply abandoned the country, the United States would lose credibility with its allies. Countries would not trust the United States to protect them if the US Army simply walked away. In theory, Vietnamization would enable the United States to leave Vietnam without appearing to lose the war.

When Nixon took office the United States still had almost 550,000 troops in Vietnam. By 1972, that number had been reduced to around 70,000. Nixon started Vietnamization in 1969 by withdrawing 25,000 troops from Vietnam. In 1970, he implemented the phased withdrawal of 150,000 more US soldiers. The South Vietnamese Army, however, could not hold off attacks from the North. With Kissinger's approval, Nixon tried to support South Vietnam through more bombing raids. The troop withdrawals were popular with the American public, but the continued bombing incurred the rage of antiwar activists. Nixon was often portrayed as no better at ending the war than Johnson had been.

Pacification and the Phoenix Program

One of the greatest challenges to the United States and South Vietnam during the war was countering the influence of the Viet Cong in the countryside. The Viet Cong recruited insurgents mostly from rural villages. Sometimes the Viet Cong conscripted people through force. Other times, villagers would volunteer to fight in the guerilla army. Those who saw the South Vietnamese government as corrupt and indifferent to the suffering of the countryside were especially ripe for Viet Cong recruitment. Some historians estimate that after the Tet Offensive slightly more than half of all rural villages in South Vietnam were under Viet Cong control. As the Viet Cong could be very elusive, this is not easy to prove. It is clear, however, that the Viet Cong held significant power in rural areas following Tet.

Pacification meant using positive means to deter people from joining the Viet Cong. Teams of American and South Vietnamese aid workers would bring food and medical supplies to rural hamlets. To counter the increase in Viet Cong-controlled hamlets after the Tet Offensive, the United States developed a program called **Civil Operations and Revolutionary Development Support (CORDS)**. CORDS brought economic aid to rural Vietnam. That aid could mean anything from establishing schools to building electric generators. The program was staffed by a combination of civilian and military personnel. These aid workers also tried to educate the local people about the value of democracy. The US press dubbed this "winning hearts and minds."

Another method of countering the Viet Cong came through gathering intelligence. Throughout the war the CIA had been involved in secret, or covert, operations to identify Viet Cong members and their strongholds. Working in coordination with South Vietnamese police, the CIA instigated the **Phoenix Program**. Anyone accused of belonging to or aiding the Viet Cong could be arrested, interrogated, and jailed. If an accused person was considered an immediate threat or resisted arrest he or she could be executed without trial. The program had little supervision from the American government. Abuses proliferated. Little proof of guilt was needed for an arrest or execution to take place. People could accuse neighbors in order to settle old scores. Once arrested, the accused might provide false information to avoid torture. Anyone critical of the government for any reason could be branded Viet Cong and killed. The Phoenix program had its defenders, who claimed that many of those arrested and killed were indeed Viet Cong. They also pointed out that the tactics of the CIA were no different from those used by the Viet Cong itself who often tortured and murdered anyone suspected of cooperating with the United States.

Any success the Phoenix Program may have had is difficult to measure, as no one knows how many of those targeted were actually Viet Cong. Approximately 80,000 people were arrested. Between 26,000 and 40,000 may have been killed. When the program finally became public, people were outraged. Reports of Americans condoning and even participating in torture and cold-blooded murder seemed yet another indication that the war in Vietnam was destroying the integrity of the United States. After a series of congressional hearings, the CIA officially terminated the program in 1972. However, the process of interrogating and executing suspected Viet Cong continued under the auspices of the South Vietnamese government until the end of the war.

My Lai and the Deterioration of the US Military

On March 16, 1968, US soldiers of Charlie Company, part of the 11th Infantry Brigade, entered the village of My Lai. The men allegedly had orders to find and eliminate any Viet Cong suspects and destroy the village. By the time the US troops left later that day, around 500 villagers lay dead, many of them women and children. Some of the bodies had been beaten and tortured; many were mutilated. According to reports that emerged later, My Lai was a peaceful village with no serious connection to the Viet Cong. The soldiers had searched the huts and found only three weapons. The villagers offered no resistance. Instead of ordering his men to leave, Lt. William Calley, the commanding officer, told the villagers to line up in groups. He then ordered his men to execute them. When some of the men hesitated, Calley himself started shooting. The soldiers burned huts. Anyone found hiding was dragged out and killed. Women were sexually assaulted.

The massacre finally stopped when helicopter pilot Warrant Officer Hugh Thompson landed his helicopter between the soldiers and the villagers. He had seen the piles of dead bodies while he was flying overhead and suspected something was wrong. Thompson and his two-man crew threatened to shoot their fellow American soldiers if they did not retreat. Finally, the soldiers left the villagers alone. Thompson flew many wounded survivors to hospitals.

The Army tried to cover up the massacre, but rumors reached the United States. Seymour Hersh, a journalist, investigated reports of an "incident" in My Lai. His main source was Vietnam veteran Ron Ridenhour. Although Ridenhour had not participated in My Lai, he was assigned to the 11th Brigade in Vietnam and had spoken to many who had taken part. After returning to the United States, he wrote letters to US government officials alerting them to the massacre. None responded to him. Hersh's finished article ran in several major newspapers in November 1969. Unable to deny the massacre any longer, the Army launched its own investigation into My Lai. Twenty-eight officers were charged with either committing crimes at My Lai or participating in an illegal cover-up of those crimes. In the end, only Lt. Calley received a sentence. Calley claimed he was following the orders of his senior officer who had told him to destroy the village and its residents. Though sentenced to life in prison, Calley served only three days. He appealed his sentence and was officially paroled in 1974. After being ostracized by the Army for decades, Thompson and his crew received Soldiers Medals in 1998.

The news of the My Lai massacre changed how Americans saw the military. People were both angered and saddened by what they heard. More reports emerged of immoral and brutal acts committed by US soldiers in Vietnam. The Army seemed to have no discipline, direction, or goal. Soldiers were not fighting for freedom or to defend democracy. Killing people had become an end in itself. It is important to note that not all soldiers engaged in atrocities or supported those who did. The actions of a few, though, tainted all returning veterans. The war in Vietnam was increasingly something that most Americans wanted to put behind them.

Secret Negotiations (1969–1971)

In February 1970, Henry Kissinger began a series of secret peace negotiations with Le Duc Tho of North Vietnam. The secret talks were an attempt to break a stalemate that had developed at the Paris Peace Talks. North Vietnam wanted the United States to replace South Vietnam's President Nguyen Van Thieu with someone they found more cooperative. The United States refused. The United States wanted North Vietnam to cease all activity in Laos and Cambodia before US troops withdrew completely. North Vietnam refused. Despite these difficulties, the two sides were coming closer to a final agreement. While they negotiated, the military conflict continued. Nevertheless, both sides recognized that the war was coming to an end. In 1973, Kissinger and Tho received the Nobel Peace Prize for their work in helping reach a peace settlement in Vietnam.

The 1972 Spring Offensive

In March 1972, North Vietnam launched an offensive. The action was intended to place the North in as strong a position as possible when American troops finally withdrew. The size and strength of the attack surprised both the United States and South Vietnam. For once, North Vietnam did not rely on guerilla warfare with its sudden attacks and retreats by small, highly mobile cadres. The **Spring Offensive** was more in keeping with traditional warfare. Large battalions of North Vietnamese soldiers invaded the South from three directions. They used tanks and heavy artillery. The United States supported the South Vietnamese Army with air strikes. The offensive was something of a test for Vietnamization. It was the first time the South Vietnamese Army had to fight off a major onslaught on its own. The South Vietnamese Army did succeed in routing the Northern forces in some areas, especially in and around the city of Hue. However, the North gained control of much of the northern region of South Vietnam near the border. Both sides suffered heavy losses. The North had won territory but paid a steep price. The South had fought far better than expected, but still suffered from disorganization. The Paris Peace talks continued throughout the Offensive. Neither side truly wanted to continue the war.

The October Agreement

In October 1972, North Vietnam made a major concession in the Paris Peace Talks. The North would no longer demand the United States replace President Thieu of South Vietnam. In return for this concession they asked that North Vietnamese troops be allowed to remain in South Vietnam after the signing of the agreement. Kissinger felt that a peace deal was close. This was welcome news to Nixon, who was running for re-election in 1972. A peace treaty was drawn up on October 12, but Thieu refused to sign an agreement that left northern soldiers in the south. He felt he had been cut out of the negotiations by Kissinger's secret talks with Tho. Angered by Thieu, North Vietnam also refused to sign the accords. The North Vietnamese accused Kissinger of lying to them.

Thieu's refusal to cooperate endangered Nixon's campaign. Nixon wanted to be able to claim peace in Vietnam. While negotiations continued, Kissinger made a public announcement declaring "peace is at hand." The announcement helped propel Nixon to a landslide victory over his Democratic opponent George McGovern. The war continued for nearly three more years.

The Christmas Bombing

By December 1972, the Paris Peace Talks were once more mired in stalemate. Angered at North Vietnam's refusal to sign the agreement, President Nixon made one last air assault to force North Vietnam to accept the treaty's conditions. During North Vietnam's Spring Offensive, Nixon had launched an air campaign called Operation Linebacker. In the winter of 1972, Operation Linebacker entered its second phase. On December 18, American B-52 aircraft began dropping bombs on Hanoi and the surrounding area. Over the next two weeks, US planes dropped more than 20,000 tons of explosives. North Vietnam claimed at least 1,600 civilian casualties. The US lost 15 B-52 bombers and 11 other aircraft. Kissinger insisted the North Vietnamese had brought the bombing on themselves by their refusal to cooperate. His critics saw the bombing as brutal and unnecessary. They believed it was simply a show of power to convince South Vietnam that they could still rely on US military might. On December 29, North Vietnam indicated its willingness to return to the negotiating table. The bombing ceased. In early 1973, the Paris Peace Accords were finally signed.

Triangular Diplomacy: the United States, the Soviet Union, and China

While he was negotiating with North Vietnam, now-Secretary of State Kissinger was also holding discussions with the Soviet Union and China. He asked the communist powers to put pressure on North Vietnam to accept the agreement. In return, they would enjoy better relations with the United States. Nixon had visited China in 1969, a major breakthrough in Sino-American relations. China no longer represented a threat but rather a potential market for US goods. Expanding trade had become more important than containing communism. China, too, would benefit from opening itself economically to the west. The United States and China did not want a proxy war in Vietnam.

The United States and the Soviet Union had also begun establishing a cautious détente. While China and the Soviet Union were officially allies, the two nations often had a difficult relationship. Kissinger thought he could exploit those difficulties to the advantage of the United States. If the two main communist nations were at odds with one another, they could not present a united front in support of North Vietnam. The Soviet Union had begun to regard North Vietnam as a burden. It had no interest in jeopardizing its own future for one small nation in Southeast Asia. Nixon offered the Soviet Union the opportunity to buy large quantities of American wheat, a major boost to the Soviet economy. In May of 1973, the United States and the Soviet Union signed a nuclear arms control treaty, another step towards détente.

Through working with China and the Soviet Union, Nixon and Kissinger could indirectly influence the peace accords. Without direct support from either China or the Soviet Union, it would be impossible for North Vietnam to continue the war.

Paris Peace Accords (1973)

On January 27, 1973, the United States, North Vietnam, South Vietnam, and the Provisional Revolutionary Government (Viet Cong) all signed the **Paris Peace Accords**. The Accords called for an immediate ceasefire throughout Vietnam. The United States would withdraw all its troops and advisors within 60 days. North Vietnam would release all prisoners of war. The ultimate goal of the Accords was the reunification of Vietnam through free and peaceful elections.

Other provisions of the Accords included the following:

- An agreement that all sides would refrain from military activities in Laos and Cambodia and withdraw any troops already there.
- The 17th parallel would serve as a border between North and South Vietnam.
- Thieu would continue to be president of South Vietnam until elections took place. North Vietnam would make no attempt to push him from office by force.
- North Vietnam would not take any aggressive action to seize territory before the elections.
- An international committee would supervise the implementation of the Accords.

Free elections never came. Although US military involvement in Vietnam was effectively over, the nation was far from at peace.

THE WAR AT HOME (1968–1972)

Campus Unrest

Throughout the 1960s and early 1970s, college campuses served as centers of the antiwar movement. In part, this was due to the draft resistance movement. College students did not want to be drafted into a war they did not support once they graduated and lost their educational deferment. In a larger sense, though, the antiwar movement on college campuses represented a change between how younger and older people perceived the role of the United States in the world. Older people who had lived through World War II sometimes condemned antiwar activists as unpatriotic. Young people accused older people of blind loyalty to a lost cause.

An organization called **Students for a Democratic Society (SDS)** took a prominent role in organizing antiwar protests. Founded in 1959, the SDS was originally dedicated to helping the civil rights movement. In 1965, the SDS organized an antiwar march in Washington, D.C. As the war escalated, the SDS became increasingly militant. Protests frequently turned violent. Confrontations between students and police disrupted college campuses.

Occupying administrative buildings became a common protest tactic. Students would stage a "sit-in" in campus offices to protest university policies. They wanted universities to sever connections with companies that made weapons for the defense department or participated in war related research. Students also wanted the **Reserve Officers Training Corps (ROTC)** banned from college campuses. ROTC enabled military volunteers to receive a college degree before entering the service full-time. ROTC candidates received stipends and attended special classes to prepare for military careers. Military recruiters visited campuses to promote ROTC. Antiwar activists thought that colleges with ROTC programs indirectly endorsed and supported the war. ROTC was eventually barred from several universities including Harvard and Yale. Most state colleges and universities continued to sponsor ROTC, so the protest was only partially successful.

Tensions between college students and local authorities reached a boiling point in 1970. On May 7, Ohio National Guardsmen were ordered to Kent State University to put down a protest. The National Guard used teargas. The protesters responded with rocks. Chaos ensued. A line of guardsmen opened fire on the crowd. Four protesters died and nine were wounded. Across the country, campuses erupted in demonstrations. On May 14, police officers killed two students and wounded 12 others at Jackson State University, a historically black college in Florida. The Kent State shootings became symbolic of the deepening rift in American society. For many, the violence and tragedy of Vietnam had truly "come home."

Peace Activists and Moratoria

The antiwar movement expanded beyond college campuses. As Americans grew weary of the long war, older people began to join the demonstrations, closing the "generation gap." When author of the bestselling book *Baby and Childcare* Dr. Benjamin Spock declared his opposition to the war, thousands of ordinary people began to rethink their position on the war. Women who had relied on Dr. Spock's book to raise their children listened to him. The women's organization Another Mother for Peace conducted a letter writing campaign urging manufacturers to sever their connections with the military. These manufacturers also made toasters, refrigerators, and other household goods. A boycott would be a major loss of income.

Peace activists also organized **moratoria**, or mass demonstrations to protest the war. The purpose of the moratoria was to bring everyday life to a halt. Sometimes the moratoria were called **strikes**, though they were not labor strikes in the ordinary sense. Moratoria organizers encouraged students to leave their classes and workers to leave their jobs to join the demonstrations. Moratoria took place on the same day in cities and towns across the nation. On October 15, 1969, thousands of people joined a nationwide Vietnam Moratorium against the war. It was the largest mass demonstration to that date and one of the largest in US history. As many as two million protestors may have participated in the October moratorium.

On November 15, around 250,000 protestors staged a moratorium march in Washington, D.C. Dr. Benjamin Spock, Senator George McGovern, and Coretta Scott King, widow of Martin Luther King Jr., were among those who gave speeches. Supporters of the war organized counter demonstrations. Some scuffles broke out, but the march was largely peaceful. The moratoria proved that millions of Americans had turned against the war and wanted it to end.

The Miami and Chicago Conventions

In 1968, the Republican Party held its political convention in Miami, Florida. The Democrats held theirs in Chicago. Both conventions attracted protests, but those in Chicago were larger and received more publicity. From August 26–29, protestors filled the streets of Chicago while Democratic Party delegates met at the city's International Amphitheater to nominate Hubert Humphrey for president. Radical activists Abbie Hoffman and Jerry Rubin staged an alternate "Yippie" convention. Chicago Mayor Richard J. Daley tried to limit the protests to Lincoln Park, the city's largest public park. He deployed police to contain the demonstrators as protests spilled out into the streets far beyond the park. The police used teargas and billy clubs to quell the demonstrations. Thousands of protestors were arrested. Despite days of protests and clashes with police, the demonstrators did not bring the convention to a halt. News footage of the violence shadowed Humphrey's campaign. Many historians believe the protests contributed to his defeat the following November.

The Republican Convention was also marked by protests. On August 7, several civil rights groups called for a rally in Liberty City, Miami's largest black neighborhood. The protests were not specifically antiwar. Demonstrators wanted to draw attention to the poor living conditions and lack of opportunities in Liberty City. The Republican Convention was meeting August 5–8 several miles away at the Miami Beach Convention Center. The demonstrators did not threaten the convention, but the police were anxious. Riots broke out in Liberty City. The police responded with tear gas. The Republican civil rights activist Ralph Abernathy left the convention to try to make peace with the protestors. He failed. In the following days, police killed three people and wounded at least one. The governor of Florida sent in the National Guard. The demonstrators disbanded. Nixon was less affected by the Liberty City protests than Humphrey was by those in Chicago and won the presidency in November.

The Counterculture, Antiwar Movement, and Silent Majority

In a speech in May 1969, Republican Vice President Spiro Agnew said, ". . . America's silent majority is bewildered by irrational protest. . ." He meant that a majority of Americans did not side with the protestors. Agnew was not the first to use the phrase "silent majority" to refer to those whose voices seem to go unheard, but his speech seemed to hit a nerve. Nixon invoked the "silent majority" on November 3, 1969 when he addressed the nation regarding the Paris Peace Talks. He deliberately distanced himself from the antiwar movement saying, "And so tonight—to you, the great silent majority of my fellow Americans—I ask for your support." Even some of those who disapproved of the war were put off by what they perceived as the growing radicalism of the antiwar left. Members of the silent majority may have opposed the war, but they wanted to do so peacefully.

The divide between Americans was not just about politics, it was about how people chose to live. The term **counterculture** referred to those outside the mainstream of American life. Young people who belonged to the counterculture explored new communities, sometimes living in communes or collectives. Unmarried couples lived together. The growing women's movement challenged the idea that being a full-time "housewife" was the right life for every woman. Recreational drugs were tolerated in the counterculture.

An article in a San Francisco newspaper called the young people of the counterculture **hippies** and the name stuck. Hippies wore different clothes, listened to different music, and used their own slang. Over the years, the ideas and lifestyles of the counterculture and the silent majority grew closer. Some counterculture ideas such as communes became marginalized but others such as equal rights for women became part of the American mainstream. Hippie clothes were sold in big department stores. Counterculture music could be heard on the radio everywhere. More importantly, organized protests became a more accepted part of the American tradition.

The Pentagon Papers

In the summer of 1971, the *New York Times* began publishing a series of articles based on a top-secret study the government had conducted of America's involvement in Vietnam since the 1940s. The articles were eye opening to most Americans. Readers learned that presidents as far back as Harry S. Truman had failed to be honest about the extent of the US commitment in Vietnam. Both Truman and Eisenhower had sent more advisors and aid to the French than previously believed. The study also revealed that Kennedy's administration had helped engineer the coup that killed South Vietnamese President Diem. Johnson had made plans to escalate the war even though he made statements to the contrary during his 1964 presidential campaign. The government study became known as the **Pentagon Papers**. The US Justice Department quickly ordered the *New York Times* and other newspapers to stop publishing the articles claiming a risk to national security. On June 30, the Supreme Court ruled in favor of the news media that the publication of the Pentagon Papers did not threaten national security. Reporters saw the ruling as victory for freedom of the press.

The *New York Times* had received the top-secret study from Daniel Ellsberg. A former US Marine, Ellsberg had been hired to work on the study as part of his job with the RAND Corporation in 1967. He started as a firm supporter of the war, but by 1969, his sympathies had shifted. What he learned and read convinced him that the war was a mistake. He also believed that the American people deserved to know the truth about their government. Ellsberg and Anthony Russo, a colleague who had helped him deliver the Pentagon Papers to the press, were arrested and charged with espionage. All charges were dropped after the government admitted to illegally wiretapping their phone conversations and even to breaking into the office of a psychiatrist Ellsberg was seeing at the time. Ellsberg went on to a career as an antiwar speaker and writer. He co-founded the Freedom of the Press Foundation in 2012.

The complete Pentagon Papers consisted of 7,000 pages of analysis and primary sources. Only a small portion was published in the 1970s. The full study was declassified and made available to the public by the National Archives and Records Administration in 2011.

CAMBODIA AND LAOS

The Geneva Accords (1954)

The **Geneva Accords** created separate agreements for Cambodia and Laos, respectively. Both nations had become independent of France in 1953 and had established constitutional monarchies. Both had strong communist factions, which would destabilize their government and create civil strife. The Accords called for a ceasefire in Laos and Cambodia, followed by free elections. The other nations agreed to respect the sovereignty and borders of Laos and Cambodia and refrain from setting up military bases in their territories. Both nations would be neutral. This neutrality soon proved impossible to maintain. Cambodia and Laos bordered on Vietnam, and as the war in Vietnam escalated, the countries were inevitably drawn into the conflict.

JFK and Laotian Neutrality (1962)

Laos rapidly collapsed into civil war after the signing of the Geneva Accords. Backed by North Vietnam, the communist faction **Pathet Lao** sought to overthrow the Royal Lao government, a government supported by the United States. President Dwight Eisenhower had sent military advisors and aid as part of his policy of containment but his efforts were not enough to shore up the Laotian government. When John F. Kennedy took office in 1961, the country seemed on the verge of a communist takeover. President Kennedy did not want to commit US ground troops to Laos because he knew it was in the best interest of the United States for Laos to remain neutral. In 1962, Kennedy called for a peace conference with representatives from the United States, the Soviet Union, Cambodia, China, North Vietnam, and several other nations. Kennedy hoped the Soviet Union would put pressure on North Vietnam to respect Laotian neutrality. The Declaration on the Neutrality of Laos established a coalition government of three parties—communist, pro-American, and neutral. The signatories of the Declaration also promised they would not interfere with the government of Laos or establish military bases there.

Hostilities in Laos resumed almost as soon as the Declaration was signed. The Pathet Lao persisted in its attacks on the government. The North Vietnamese Army had established the Ho Chi Minh Trail through parts of Laos and continued to use the route to infiltrate South Vietnam. The United States began bombing the trail to stop North Vietnam from invading the South via Laos. The US air bombardment of Laos would continue until the end of the war.

Ho Chi Minh Trail

The Ho Chi Minh Trail traveled from North Vietnam down the western border of South Vietnam to the Gulf of Thailand. Most of the trail was in Cambodia and Laos. The trail was not a single road but a network of ancient footpaths, waterways, tunnels, and old French roads and new Vietnamese ones. Branches off the main trail led into South Vietnam. The Viet Cong used the trail as a place to hide and regroup when they had to flee

US and South Vietnamese forces. Both the North Vietnamese Army and the Viet Cong stored caches of weapons, food, and other supplies along the trail. The tunnels often stretched deep into South Vietnam and served as a means of connecting the North Vietnamese Army with the Viet Cong.

The Ho Chi Minh Trail was approximately 10,000 miles long (16,000 km). Between its inception in 1959 and the end of the war in 1975, around one million soldiers moved down the trail along with tons of supplies. North Vietnam considered the maintenance of the trail a top priority. Women worked on the trail along with men. Students would be pulled out of school to repair the trail after US air strikes. Working on the Ho Chi Minh Trail would become one of the great unifying experiences of the generation that grew up during the war. The communists called the trail the "Blood Road," because so many soldiers and workers died on it. Most were victims of US bombs, but tropical diseases like malaria and accidents took many lives too. The trail was so effective that even American generals conceded it was a remarkable feat of military engineering.

The Secret War in Laos

In the early 1960s, the CIA started sending agents to arm and train Hmong tribesmen in Laos to fight against the Pathet Lao and attack transports along the Ho Chi Minh Trail. These soldiers became known as the **Secret Army**. At the time, the Hmong lived in the mountain regions of Southeast Asia. They were known for their strong sense of independence and embraced their own culture, language, and religious practices. Most of the Hmong were anticommunist, viewing communism as part of the foreign incursion from North Vietnam.

The Hmong guerilla units served under General Vang Pao, the only Hmong tribesman to achieve the rank of general in the Laotian Army. The CIA also recruited soldiers from other indigenous tribes in Laos, including the Yao and Lao Thung. Around 9,000 **Montagnards**, or mountain tribesmen, served in the Secret Army. The Secret Army fought in conjunction with the Royal Lao Army to defeat the Pathet Lao and the North Vietnamese. The United States provided air support by dropping supplies to units in mountainous areas and bombing the Ho Chi Minh Trail. American bombing began to escalate under the Johnson administration in 1964.

The civil war in Laos is often referred to as the **Secret War** because so few were aware of US activities within the nation. In many ways, the Secret War in Laos transformed the CIA. The agency was no longer devoted to simply gathering intelligence. CIA operatives acted more like a paramilitary program training recruits in military discipline and techniques. The war gave the CIA an expanded role in US defense that it continued to enlarge upon after the war was over.

Sihanouk and Cambodian Neutrality

After the French withdrew from Cambodia in 1953, Norodom Sihanouk became the constitutional monarch. Sihanouk was popular with the Cambodian people and won an election in 1955. At various times, he served as president and prime minister in addition to being king. Sihanouk tried to maintain Cambodia's neutrality, but his government was weak. A communist faction called the **Khmer Rouge** conducted a guerilla campaign against the government in the countryside. Sihanouk's policy towards North Vietnam consisted of a tacit agreement not to challenge the use of the Ho Chi Minh Trail as long as the North Vietnamese stayed in the eastern part of Cambodia and did not interfere with the rest of the country. At the same time, he privately indicated to the United States that he would not object to bombing raids on the Ho Chi Minh Trail as long as they did not kill Cambodian civilians. Sihanouk's efforts to balance the needs of both sides undermined his authority. Inevitably, civilians died. Cambodia did not enjoy true neutrality. Sihanouk became less popular.

Afraid of a communist coup, he used torture and executions to silence his enemies. Suspicious of the CIA, he refused US aid and cut off diplomatic relations with the United States. Some of his own generals no longer supported him. In an effort to regain their favor, he reinstated relations with the United States but by then, it was too late. The Americans backed another leader. In March 1970, Sihanouk's government was overthrown by a military coup while he was traveling abroad. General Lon Nol became the new head of state.

Lon Nol and the US Incursion

Although he called himself president, Lon was a dictator. He was also staunchly anticommunist. The CIA has never admitted to direct involvement in the overthrow of Sihanouk, but Lon Nol clearly had American support once he took office. His first act was to call for the withdrawal of all North Vietnamese troops. The North Vietnamese considered the Ho Chi Minh Trail their lifeline and had no intention of leaving Cambodia. Together with Viet Cong units, the North Vietnamese Army invaded Cambodia, moving deep into the country, well beyond the narrow strip of land surrounding the Ho Chi Minh Trail. The communist forces hoped they could overthrow the government and set up a communist state under the Khmer Rouge. The United States responded by launching an invasion of Cambodia.

On April 30, 1970, President Nixon publicly announced that ground troops had been deployed to Cambodia. The antiwar movement saw this as a senseless escalation of the war. North Vietnamese forces in Cambodia did not threaten US or South Vietnamese troops. Cambodia was still technically neutral. Nixon had stated that he was withdrawing US troops from Vietnam only a few weeks earlier. Now the United States seemed to be sinking into yet another unwinnable war in Southeast Asia.

Around 50,600 US servicemen participated in the **Cambodia Campaign**, along with approximately 58,000 South Vietnamese troops. The incursion into Cambodia lasted from April 29 to July 22, 1970. Most US troops were withdrawn in June. South Vietnamese units stayed another month. Cambodia was torn by civil war. The Khmer Rouge grew stronger. Lon Nol could not control the country. In the United States, Nixon faced his own political challenges from the left. His bombing campaign over Cambodia and Laos would only add to the dissent.

The Secret Bombing of Laos and Cambodia

From March 1969 to August 1973, the United States carried out two bombing campaigns targeting Cambodia and Laos: **Operation Menu**, which lasted from March 1969 to May 1970, and **Operation Freedom Deal**, which extended from May 1970 to August 1973. President Johnson had ordered bombing raids on Cambodia as early as 1964. Nixon's campaigns, however, represented a significant escalation of the air war. Under Nixon, the bombing extended far beyond the Ho Chi Minh Trail into the central regions of Laos and Cambodia. Nixon called for the use of B-52 planes that could deliver a large "payload" of explosives with each fight. He also ordered carpet, or saturation, bombing. **Carpet-bombing** means that planes drop as many bombs as possible over a given area in a short period of time. They do not target specific structures, buildings, or installations. The bombs are meant to make an entire area useless and uninhabitable. Nixon intended to support his policy of Vietnamization. The bombing would make it impossible for Viet Cong and North Vietnamese soldiers to hide in Cambodia and Laos, giving an edge to the South Vietnamese forces after the United States withdrew.

During the war in Vietnam, US planes dropped around 2.7 million tons of bombs on Cambodia and 2 million tons on Laos. By contrast, the US dropped approximately 2.1 million bombs on Europe and Asia during all of World War II. Laos received more bombs per person than any other country in history.

While most Americans knew about the land incursion into Cambodia, few civilians outside of Nixon's inner circle were aware of the extensive bombing campaign. Only five senators were briefed. In December 1972, Senator William Proxmire received a letter from an ex-serviceman who had participated in the bombing. The serviceman wondered if the raids were legal. Did the president have the authority to order air strikes against two countries that had never threatened the United States or its military? Proxmire began to ask questions. In 1973, the Senate Armed Services Committee held a series of hearings on the bombing in Southeast Asia. Military officers and government officials testified. The information they gave was limited by security issues. The full extent of the bombing campaigns would not be known until many years after the war. What the senators did hear was enough to convince them that Nixon had deliberately misled and lied to the American people about his military policies in Vietnam.

The Senate hearing attracted the attention of the press. Once more, the public felt betrayed by the government. The bombing raids made the United States look like a wanton aggressor, not a protector of freedom. People were especially alarmed by the military's use of cluster bombs, which are small bombs designed to explode into shrapnel and cause as many casualties as possible.

Although the intention was to make it impossible for Viet Cong and North Vietnamese soldiers to hide in Cambodia and Laos, the bombardments also made it impossible for civilians to live in the countryside. In Laos, people hid caves in the mountains. In Cambodia, thousands sought refuge in the city of Phnom Penh.

The Khmer Rouge and the Fall of Phnom Penh (1975)

As the United States withdrew its forces from the region, the communist Khmer Rouge faction in Cambodia ramped up its assaults on rural towns and villages. North Vietnam was busy preparing for its last push to take over the South and had ceased to actively support the Khmer Rouge. Even without aid, the Cambodian guerilla force managed to seize almost 60 percent of Cambodia's land by 1973. The long civil war coupled with the

American bombing campaign had left Lon Nol's government in chaos. The Khmer Rouge employed brutal tactics. When they took over a village, they insisted on total obedience. Anyone who questioned authority or bent rules was executed. The Khmer Rouge was antireligion. Most Cambodians were Buddhist. The Khmer Rouge drove Buddhist monks from their monasteries. Those who resisted were tortured and killed. More refugees crowded into Phnom Penh as the advancing Khmer Rouge surrounded the city.

In January 1975, the Khmer Rouge launched a final assault on Phnom Penh. After a siege of four months, the city fell on April 17. Lon Nol surrendered. The Khmer Rouge leader Pol Pot took over the government. Under the Khmer Rouge, Cambodia became cut off from the outside world. Few foreigners were allowed into the country and citizens were rarely permitted to leave. The country became a prison camp. Arrest, torture, and execution were common. Private property was forbidden. Urban people were forced to abandon their homes to farm in the countryside. They had no experience working the land. Starvation spread.

Historians consider the Cambodian deaths under the Khmer Rouge to be genocide. Between 13 to 30 percent of the total population, or between 1.2 and 2.8 million people, died. The actual number is unknown. In 1978, Vietnam invaded Cambodia and overthrew the Khmer Rouge. The country slowly managed to reconstruct itself. In 1997, Cambodia set up the Khmer Rouge War Crimes Tribunal with the help of the United Nations. Pol Pot died in 1998 before he could face the tribunal.

The Communist Victory in Laos

After signing the Paris Peace Accords, the three major factions in Laos (the right-wing Lao Issara, the communist Pathet Lao, and a neutral third faction) signed their own treaty, the **Vientiane Agreement**, in February 1973. The Agreement set up a coalition government under the leadership of Prime Minister Souvanna Phouma. North Vietnamese troops still occupied Laos, as the Paris Accords did not require them to withdraw. North Vietnam supported the Pathet Lao. Without American aid, the Royal Lao government could not oppose communism. The Pathet Lao became the leading political party. In 1975, the Pathet Lao overthrew the monarchy and declared the country to be the Lao People's Democratic Republic. The Republic was guided and largely controlled by communist Vietnam. The communist policy of establishing agriculture collectives did appeal to peasants who had always worked on family farms. Laos remained poor for many years, and food was scarce. Nearly 10 percent of the population fled between 1975 and 1985. In 1986, the government introduced reforms. A new constitution granted citizens a limited amount of freedom to travel. Private property was permitted once more. Laos began encouraging foreign investments. The nation became a full member of the World Trade Organization in 2013.

"A DECENT INTERVAL"

The Ceasefire Violations

The Paris Peace Accords called for a ceasefire in Vietnam that would set the stage for a lasting peace. In private, Henry Kissinger, the US architect of the accords, acknowledged that South Vietnam would eventually fall to the North. Vietnamization had failed. South Vietnam had neither the political nor military power to fight off an invasion from the North without US help. Kissinger hoped that South Vietnam would stay independent for at least two or three years. He referred to this as "a decent interval" in his notes. He did not want the international community to think the United States had abandoned South Vietnam to the communists. He also did not want the US withdrawal to look like a defeat. Like Kissinger, Nixon agreed that South Vietnam would not be able to fend off the North. In public, he proclaimed that peace had finally come to Vietnam.

Neither North nor South Vietnam wanted a complete ceasefire. Both sides wanted to seize as much territory as possible before the accords were signed on January 27, 1973. Fighting continued even after the accords. The South Vietnamese government still felt threatened by the Viet Cong and sought to eliminate any communist enclaves in the South. The North continued to rebuild the Ho Chi Minh Trail. In 1974, the North Vietnam conducted a series of raids to regain territory it had lost in 1973. The South Vietnamese Army successfully repulsed the North on several occasions. Without material aid from the United States, though, South Vietnamese resources were limited.

Watergate and Nixon's Resignation

By 1973, Nixon had become mired in the **Watergate Scandal**. During the presidential campaign of 1972, police had arrested several men who had broken into Democratic Party Headquarters housed in the Watergate complex in Washington, D.C. They had come to wiretap phones and steal documents. The men had connections to the Republican Committee to Reelect the President. At first, Nixon claimed no knowledge of the crime. Further investigations revealed that he was deeply involved. The investigations also uncovered the fact that Nixon recorded all his telephone conversations. The tapes implicated him in the Watergate crime. They also gave Congress and the public a glimpse into some of the more unsavory aspects of Nixon's presidency. They revealed him as both a hypocrite and a liar. On August 8, 1973, Nixon resigned from the presidency. Vice President Gerald Ford took his place.

Nixon was the first US president in history to resign from office. Although the Watergate Scandal was not related to Vietnam, the crime and Nixon's downfall seemed to symbolize a kind of moral rot in American politics and society. Many people traced that rot to the war in Vietnam. After Watergate, Americans distanced themselves from both the war and Nixon. They wanted the Vietnam era to be over once and for all.

Congressional Passage of the War Powers Act

The 1964 Gulf of Tonkin Resolution had given the president wide power to deploy the US military in Southeast Asia without consulting Congress. In effect, the Resolution let both Johnson and Nixon conduct a war almost singlehandedly. Congress never formally declared war against North Vietnam, yet the United States had been fighting in the region for nearly two decades. Fearful that a similar situation might arise in the future, Congress passed the **War Powers Act** in November 1973. The Act placed two major limitations on the president's power to deploy the military. It stipulated that the president must notify Congress within 48 hours of sending US military forces into any foreign country and that president must withdraw those forces within 60 days if Congress does not declare war or authorize further involvement. The Act also states that the president must consult with Congress before taking military action whenever possible.

Nixon vetoed the War Powers Act. Congress overturned his veto. The War Powers Act has been challenged as unconstitutional many times since its passage. Critics argue that it places restrictions on the president's power as commander in chief and endangers the safety of the nation. Supporters claim the Act prevents another Vietnam. As of 2019, the War Power Act has not been reversed. Even with the restrictions imposed by the Act, the president still has wide latitude to deploy the military abroad.

The Great Spring Offensive

In March 1975, North Vietnam launched a final offensive against South Vietnam. The North Vietnamese government knew that the United States would not come to the aid of the South. Congress had made it clear that the US would no longer supply men, ammunition, or air power to South Vietnam. The objective of the offensive was to capture the capital city of Saigon and unite Vietnam under one communist regime. The "decent interval" was over.

The North Vietnamese started the offensive by invading the Central Highlands. Although the South Vietnamese Army had fought well before, it quickly collapsed in the face of a major invasion. Soldiers lost confidence in their officers. Their retreat was chaotic and panic-stricken. Emboldened, the North Vietnamese pressed their attack from the north, west, and south. By the middle of April, the South Vietnamese Army had been completely routed. North Vietnamese troops encircled Saigon.

The Fall of Saigon

North Vietnam had originally planned to invade Saigon in 1976. Their rapid victories, however, convinced them that they did not need to wait. They called their final push the **Ho Chi Minh Campaign**. The North Vietnamese attacked Saigon on April 29, 1975. At the time, the city was crammed with refugees. The only way out was by air or boat. The United States had already airlifted around 112,000 people, including 2,000 orphans, from South Vietnam but thousands of others still waited for evacuation. Anyone known to have connections with the United States would be automatically targeted by the North Vietnamese invaders. President Thieu resigned in anger. He accused the US of having tricked him into signing a peace agreement that only sealed South Vietnam's fate.

The United States had maintained its embassy in Saigon after the signing of the peace accords. Hundreds of people crowded onto the embassy grounds hoping to be airlifted out of the country. About 1,250 Americans remained in Vietnam, most of them attached to the embassy. On April 29, helicopters from US Navy aircraft carriers rescued around 8,000 people, including 7,000 Vietnamese civilians. South Vietnamese pilots also participated in the rescue operation. In the early morning hours of April 30, two US Marines assigned to the embassy were killed in an attack at a nearby airport. They were the last Americans to die in the war in Vietnam.

Graham Martin, the American ambassador, left Vietnam via helicopter only hours before the North Vietnamese Army entered the city. The North Vietnamese tanks rolled into Saigon. The army took the presidential palace and declared victory on April 30, 1975. The South Vietnamese government no longer existed. The Americans were gone. Vietnam had been united. The war was at last over.

US LEGACIES AND LESSONS

Impact of the War on Vietnam

The war devastated Vietnam economically and socially. Around two million civilians died in the war. Approximately 1.1 million North Vietnamese and Viet Cong soldiers died. Around 250,000 South Vietnamese soldiers were also killed. In addition, the country had to cope with many wounded and disabled people. Food and medical supplies were scarce. Herbicides like Agent Orange destroyed agricultural areas. People exposed to Agent Orange also had a high risk of having children with serious birth defects. Cities were reduced to rubble by repeated bombardments. Roads, dams, bridges, and ports were in ruins. In the ten years following the war, the country struggled economically.

Many people tried to flee by boat. Thousands of Vietnamese risked death at sea rather than remain in a country that seemed unlivable. These "boat people" were beset by pirates, starvation, and thirst. Those who survived often spent years in refugee camps before being resettled. In 1980, about 231,000 Vietnamese immigrants lived in the United States. Within ten years, that number more than doubled to 543,000. The number of Vietnamese immigrants has grown steadily every decade since then. Other Vietnamese refugees settled in Canada, Australia, Korea, Great Britain, and France. Vietnamese culture has spread throughout the world.

In 1986, the communist government of Vietnam introduced reforms allowing private property and business. Vietnam has evolved into a combination of capitalism and collectivism. The economy has slowly recovered. As of 2019, Vietnam is the world's third largest exporter of rice and second largest exporter of coffee based on the dollar value of exports. Other exports include rubber, oil, fish, and coal. Vietnam also manufactures textiles, electronic products, and many other small goods. The United States and China are the nation's two largest trading partners.

The Impact of the Vietnam Syndrome on American Foreign Policy

The term **Vietnam syndrome** has been used to describe a general reluctance on the part of the United States to become involved in foreign wars, especially with regard to committing ground troops. In the wake of Vietnam, the American public began to feel isolationist. They did not want to see American lives lost by taking sides in the affairs of other nations. Rather than a war against a communist aggressor, the war in Vietnam was seen as an internal conflict that the United States should have avoided. "Let them settle their own problems," was the overall sentiment. Politicians followed suit and ran campaigns that focused on domestic issues rather than foreign policy. Americans wanted their government to take care of problems at home.

This does not mean that the United States avoided foreign conflicts altogether. Between August 1990 and February 1991, President George H.W. Bush oversaw the Persian Gulf War. The war started when Iraqi troops invaded Kuwait. US forces quickly routed the Iraqis during Operation Desert Shield and Desert Storm. The success of the operations led many Americans to feel that the country had finally "recovered" from Vietnam. The Persian Gulf War, however, was short lived and the United States did not remain in the region. During the Kosovo War in Eastern Europe (1998–1999), President Bill Clinton conducted an air campaign in conjunction with NATO forces. The campaign was brief, and the United States did not send ground troops to fight in the region.

After the terrorist attacks on 9/11, the United States entered into two wars in the Middle East, one in Afghanistan and the other in Iraq. While Americans overwhelmingly supported a military response to the attacks, the shadow of Vietnam fell over both engagements. The wars lasted longer than expected and the results of the American efforts are still inconclusive. The memory of Vietnam continues to haunt the United States into the first decades of the twenty-first century.

The Experience of Returning Vets

Soldiers returning from Vietnam found themselves in a country that was not eager to hear their stories. Unlike World War II veterans, those who fought in Vietnam were not regarded as victorious heroes. They often bore the burden of American shame. Many suffered from **post-traumatic stress disorder (PTSD)**, a psychological condition that could include a wide range of symptoms, including depression, anxiety, and panic attacks. The Veterans Administration medical system did not always have the resources to help. Because many soldiers came from lower-income backgrounds, they struggled with lack of education and unemployment. The military had not provided them with the necessary skills to adjust to civilian life. Drug problems, alcoholism, and homelessness plagued many of the veterans. Some suffered from the effects of Agent Orange.

Many Vietnam veterans took advantage of the **G.I. Bill**, which helped veterans attend college. Vietnam veterans succeeded in many careers, including politics. Senator John McCain of Arizona served as a pilot in Vietnam. He had also been a prisoner of war. McCain used his high-profile status to advocate for Vietnam veterans. He died of cancer in 2018.

Economic Consequences

The war in Vietnam had a negative impact on the US economy. President Johnson's attempt to provide "guns and butter" led to inflation and higher taxes. The huge investment in military spending diverted industries from producing consumer goods. The government developed a budget deficit that created more inflation. Foreign trade slowed as the United States was not exporting goods for consumer markets overseas. The economy began to stagnate. Nixon tried to solve some of these problems by instituting wage and price controls. His economic policies were not popular. Employers laid off workers rather than meet wage standards. Merchants protested that price controls cut into their profits. Consumers grew cautious, unsure of what might happen next. With fewer sales, businesses could not expand.

Nixon also took the United States off the gold standard. Once US currency was no longer backed by gold, the value of the dollar fell. This development contributed to the OPEC oil embargo of 1973. The oil-producing nations of the Middle East sold millions of barrels of oil to the United States. They declared an embargo on sales to the United States to protest the declining value of the dollar. The United States went into an economic recession and did not fully recover until the 1980s. As important as any specific economic effects was the feeling the Vietnam had drained the country and sapped its emotional energy. The legacy of Vietnam War reached into every aspect of American life.

The Impact on the US Military

In 1973, Congress ended the draft. The military would henceforth rely on an all-volunteer force. This was in part due to the antidraft protests. Improvements in weapons and technology also meant that fewer soldiers were needed to conduct war. After Vietnam, the military became more heavily invested in air weapons and special operations teams rather than ground troops. Air bombardments require fewer personnel. The military also had to face the fact that an enemy with inferior weapons, less equipment, and poorer supplies had foiled the greatest military power in the world.

The US Defense Department never developed any single consensus on what went wrong. Some officers blamed the media and Congress, still believing that with enough support on the home front the United States could have won the war. Other analysts concluded that the United States lacked clear goals from the beginning. Winning had never been defined. Soldiers did not know what they were fighting for or against.

The military was often ambivalent about reports of atrocities in Vietnam, including the massacre at My Lai. On one hand, My Lai encouraged deep soul searching. On the other, it led to denial. The military instituted policies aimed at preventing the mistreatment of civilians. Whether or not those policies were enforced, however, depended on the commitment of commanding officers.

After Vietnam, Americans tended to be "risk averse" in war. People did not want to deal with the loss of American lives. In Vietnam, soldiers increasingly received medals and honors not for killing the enemy but for saving the lives of their fellow Americans in battle. The American public was more interested in seeing its soldiers come home alive than it was in hearing about dead opponents. As a consequence, the military sought ways to minimize casualties.

Above all, Vietnam taught the military the value of public perception. The media played an important role in Vietnam. Those who controlled the story controlled the war.

The Impact on the Media

Vietnam gave the media a larger role in shaping public opinion and public policy. Critics of the media often blame newspapers and television for the loss of the war. They claim that negative press reports about Vietnam turned Americans against the war. However, it is equally true that the media may have reflected what people already believed. Early protests against Vietnam were not well covered. Only when demonstration had become sizable events did they receive attention. Much of the media was harshly critical of the war in 1972, yet Nixon won re-election over George McGovern, the Democratic "peace" candidate. The media alone could not dictate how people voted. Negative press reports on the war emerged in the late 1960s. The war, however, continued until 1975. If, as some people claim, the press stopped the war, it did not do so fast enough for others.

This does not negate the fact that images and words still wielded a powerful influence. During World War II, the media had been almost entirely supportive of the US war effort. The government and the military had never had to face an antagonistic media. During the war in Vietnam, the media prompted Americans to ask questions of their elected officials and seek answers. Journalists reporting on Vietnam insisted their highest loyalty was to the truth, not to any government, even their own. Again, critics would claim that reporters had an agenda and were less than fair. The issue of how much influence the media had on the course of the war has never been fully settled. It can be said, though, that the war gave journalists a deeper appreciation of the media's power in American culture and life.

POWs and MIAs

Nixon had agreed to withdraw US troops within 60 days of signing the Paris Peace Accords if North Vietnam took immediate steps to release all American **prisoners of war (POWs)**. The first group of POWs arrived in the United States on February 12, 1973. The first group consisted of POWs who had been in captivity the longest, and those who needed urgent medical attention. Over several weeks, the North Vietnamese released a total of 591 men. Most had been pilots captured when their planes went down. Many had been held in an infamous prison they dubbed the "Hanoi Hilton." Prisoners were often held in isolation, tortured, and deprived of sleep, food, water, and light. The group remained resilient. They devised ways to communicate with one another through tap codes and other secret signals. Whenever possible they cared for each other physically and gave one another moral support. It was the prisoners themselves who decided they should be released in order of how long they had been held.

After all POWs had come home, the Defense Department compiled a list of 2,646 men who were **missing in action (MIA)** in Vietnam, Laos, and

Cambodia. Missing in action usually referred to a soldier who had died but whose remains had not been recovered. The dense jungle terrain often made it difficult to locate and retrieve bodies. Although there were reports of US soldiers alive in the region, those reports were never substantiated. In the mid-1980s, Vietnam sought better relations with the west and began to repatriate the remains of American service members. Cambodia and Laos followed suit. By 2015, the remains of 1,059 servicemen had been identified and returned the United States for burial. The Defense Department still lists the remaining 1,588 as MIA.

Collective National Amnesia

Historians sometimes refer to a collective national amnesia in the United States in the aftermath of the war. Americans did not literally forget the war, but it faded from public discourse. Most politicians did not refer to Vietnam in their campaigns. The media focused on other issues. Veterans rarely spoke about their experiences in public. The United States had no way of dealing with defeat. Americans wanted to move on to other things.

The memory of the war was not entirely lost, however. Artists, filmmakers, and writers kept the memory of Vietnam alive. In 1978, the Academy of Motion Pictures gave the award for best picture to *The Deer Hunter*, a somber look at the lives of three men from a small town who volunteer for Vietnam. Francis Ford Coppola's *Apocalypse Now*, released the following year, seemed to convey all the controversy and insanity of the war. Coppola won the Oscar for best director from the Academy. *Apocalypse Now* has become one of the most discussed, analyzed, and widely viewed films in American history.

Tim O'Brian, a Vietnam vet, received the National Book Award for his novel *Going After Cacciato*, which was based on his experiences in Vietnam. O'Brian also published a book of short stories about the war in Vietnam, *The Things They Carried,* in 1990. The book has been translated into several languages. To date, it has sold around two million copies. *The Things They Carried* has become required reading in many US high schools.

SUMMING IT UP

Vietnam Before War

- Despite a strong independent streak, Vietnam had been first a Chinese, then a French colony until 1955.
- In 1925, Nguyen Ai Quoc (who changed his name to **Ho Chi Minh**) formed the Revolutionary Youth League, later known as the **Vietnamese Communist Party**.
- In 1940, following the Japanese invasion of Vietnam and **Indochina** (French-controlled Vietnam), Ho organized guerilla fighters known as the **Viet Minh**. Following WWII, the Viet Minh fought against French soldiers during the First Indochina War.
- In 1953, French forces seized **Dien Bien Phu**, a valley along the Laos-Vietnam border. The following year, Viet Minh forces attacked and overwhelmed the French. The 1954 Geneva Conference resulted in the **Final Declaration,** dividing Vietnam into two separate nations along the 17th Parallel with plans to unify the two under a freely elected government in 1956.
- In 1955, **Ngo Dinh Diem** took control of South Vietnam. Diem was staunchly Roman Catholic and took steps to repress the Buddhist majority population, angering many South Vietnamese and opening a door to North Vietnamese interference. That anger led to the formation of the communist **National Liberation Front**, better known as the **Viet Cong**. In 1963, a group of South Vietnamese Army generals, with assistance from the Central Intelligence Agency (CIA), staged a coup and assassinated Diem and his brother Ngo Dinh Nhu.

War in Vietnam

- **Guerilla warfare** calls for small groups of soldiers to strike at vulnerable targets wherever they might be. As a result, seizing or controlling territory was not a practical way to measure victory. Through Gen. Westmoreland's strategy of attrition, US forces would instead rely on **body counts** to chart progress in Vietnam.
- The **Ho Chi Minh Trail** was a route from North Vietnam, through Laos and Cambodia, that allowed arms and supplies to flow from the North into Viet Cong hands. Despite repeated attacks, the Ho Chi Minh Trail remained a vital pipeline for North Vietnam's offensives in the South.
- North Vietnamese and Viet Cong fighters were highly disciplined and had years of experience in guerilla warfare.

- American soldiers deployed to Vietnam were often in their late teens; many had never left home before. Americans were better fed, better equipped, and had better medical care. They were also deployed for just one year. The short deployment meant soldiers focused less on their missions and more on how many days were left before going home.
- South Vietnamese civilians were often trapped between the Viet Cong and American forces. The Viet Cong would often confiscate supplies, conscript villagers, and torture or execute anyone suspected of working with the Americans. The Americans were little better; since the Viet Cong had no uniforms, many American servicemen saw everyone as potential collaborators. This included women and children, whom the Americans would suspect of carrying messages and hiding weapons. As a result, American forces would often shoot indiscriminately, killing civilians they thought to be Viet Cong.
- South Vietnamese people living in cities such as Saigon profited through drugs, prostitution, and a black market reselling American goods to Vietnamese civilians. Other Vietnamese sought more legitimate sources of income, working in the US Embassy or as translators and guides for American journalists.
- **Pacification** was an effort by the US and South Vietnamese militaries to prevent rural villages from siding with the Viet Cong. This effort saw aid workers bringing food and medical supplies to the countryside villages. Further efforts included building schools and providing electric generators, under the mantle of "**winning hearts and minds**" of the South Vietnamese people.
- The **Phoenix Program** was a cooperative program involving the CIA and South Vietnamese police in capturing, interrogating, and torturing suspected Viet Cong sympathizers. Little evidence was needed to prompt an arrest.

Beyond Vietnam

- **Cambodia** and **Laos** together form the western border of Vietnam and were eventually drawn into the war. The Ho Chi Minh Trail wound through parts of both Cambodia and Laos, making the two nations targets for communists and Americans.
- In the early 1960s, the CIA began training and arming a **secret army** of Hmong and other Laotian tribesmen in the mountains of Laos. These **Montagnards**, or mountain tribesmen, fought alongside the Laotian government against the North Vietnamese, targeting the communist Pathet Lao as well as transports along the Ho Chi Minh Trail.
- **Norodom Sihanouk** came to power in Cambodia following the French withdrawal in 1953. Sihanouk allowed North Vietnam free use of the Ho Chi

Minh Trail so long as they left the rest of Cambodia alone. His government was overthrown in a coup in 1970.

- In March 1970, Cambodian general **Lon Nol** assumed power following a coup. Lon was anticommunist, and his first official act was to order all North Vietnamese out of Cambodia. The North Vietnamese, along with Viet Cong units, invaded Cambodia to protect the Ho Chi Minh Trail. That invasion led to President Nixon deploying close to 51,000 US forces into Cambodia. South Vietnam also took part, sending an additional 58,000 soldiers to take part in the **Cambodia Campaign**.
- The **Khmer Rouge** was a communist guerilla faction in Cambodia, fighting against the Cambodian government in the countryside. Under leader Pol Pot, the Khmer Rouge took control of Cambodia in 1975, after US forces had withdrawn from the region.

Key Events in the Vietnam War

- American military advisors were in South Vietnam as early as 1950.
- Between May and December 1961, President Kennedy increased the US military presence from 400 US Army Special Forces (**Green Berets**) soldiers to more than 16,000 troops.
- In 1962, US aircraft were spraying **Agent Orange**, a powerful herbicide that destroyed thousands of acres of vegetation. Agent Orange contained harmful chemicals that affected animals and humans as well as plants: reports of birth defects, illnesses such as cancer, and even death have since been linked to Agent Orange exposure.
- By 1964, President Johnson increased the US military presence to 23,000 troops, due largely to the instability of the South Vietnamese government following Diem's assassination.
- **Gen. William Westmoreland** took command of US forces in Vietnam in 1964. Gen. Westmoreland thought little of the South Vietnamese Army, believing it fell to the United States to defeat the North. Westmoreland utilized a strategy of **attrition warfare**, consisting of relentless air and ground attacks to wear the North Vietnamese and Viet Cong forces down. Rather than controlling territory, the US strategy amounted to killing as many enemy combatants as possible.
- In early August 1964, President Johnson received word that two US Navy destroyers, the USS *Maddox* and the USS *Turner Joy*, had been attacked by North Vietnamese torpedo boats in the Gulf of Tonkin. The US responded with the **Gulf of Tonkin Resolution**, which gave Johnson almost unlimited power to wage war.

- **Operation Flaming Dart** was an American bombing campaign against North Vietnamese military targets that ran from February 7-24, 1965. The bombings were coordinated with South Vietnamese Air Force attacks on North Vietnamese outposts along the border. In March 1965, **Operation Rolling Thunder** saw US Air Force bombers attacking North Vietnamese targets along the 19th Parallel, gradually pushing north.
- Secret bombing campaigns targeting Laos and Cambodia ran from 1969 to 1973. The campaigns were codenamed **Operation Menu** (1969–1970) and **Operation Freedom Deal** (1970–1973). Under Nixon, the bombings targeted more than just the Ho Chi Minh Trail, **carpet-bombing** locations in central Laos and Cambodia to render those areas uninhabitable.
- American combat troops first arrived in Vietnam in March 1965 when President Johnson dispatched 3,500 US Marines to Vietnam. With these troops, the US could take part in offensive ground operations. By July 1965, President Johnson had ordered the deployment of an additional 100,000 troops to Vietnam.
- November 1965 saw the first significant battle between the US forces and the North Vietnamese at **Ia Drang Valley**. From November 14-16, roughly 1,000 American soldiers fought against a North Vietnamese force twice that size. The American forces managed to kill 1,500 and wound another 500 North Vietnamese soldiers while suffering only 250 dead and 245 wounded. Ia Drang also marked the first major use of helicopters in combat.
- On January 31, 1968, communist forces launched the **Tet Offensive**, attacking more than 120 separate sites throughout South Vietnam. Targets ranged from small hamlets to major cities. The Tet Offensive lasted three days and, while considered unsuccessful, struck a psychological victory against the South.
- The My Lai Massacre occurred on March 16, 1968 when soldiers from the 11th Infantry Brigade entered the village of My Lai in search of Viet Cong. Despite finding no serious connection to the Viet Cong, soldiers destroyed the village and murdered close to 500 villagers. **Lt. William Calley**, the unit commander at My Lai, was the only one out of 28 officers implicated to be punished for the massacre. He served three days in a military prison before being paroled.
- In March 1972, North Vietnamese forces launched their **Spring Offensive** to position themselves in anticipation of a US withdrawal. The offensive was a return to more traditional military tactics rather than guerilla warfare, with the use of armor and artillery to support battalions of soldiers as they attacked key targets in the south.

- The December 1972 **Christmas Bombing** of North Vietnam was an attempt to break a stalemate after North Vietnam initially refused to sign the Paris Peace Accords. The bombings did bring North Vietnam back to the negotiation table.
- The **Paris Peace Accords** were signed in January 1973 by the United States, North Vietnam, South Vietnam, and the Provisional Revolutionary Government (Viet Cong). The agreement called for an immediate cease fire, withdrawal of all US troops and advisors within 60 days, and that North Vietnam release all prisoners of war. The Accords re-established the 17th Parallel as a border and called for unification through free, peaceful elections.
- In March 1975, North Vietnam launched the **Great Spring Offensive**. The objective was to take the southern city of Saigon and unite Vietnam under communist rule. Southern Vietnamese military units collapsed under the onslaught of northern forces. Saigon fell on April 30, 1975.
- The **Ho Chi Minh Campaign** was the name for the final push by North Vietnamese forces into Saigon. The campaign was originally planned to happen in 1976, but their rapid victories led them to lay siege to Saigon earlier than expected.

Politics of War

- The 1960 election of **John F. Kennedy** brought a renewed effort to stop the spread of communism into South Vietnam. Kennedy adhered to the **Domino Theory**, an idea that as one nation fell to communism, many others would soon follow. Kennedy implemented a plan of counterinsurgency, using US forces to train and aid the South Vietnamese Army in its struggle against the communist north and southern Viet Cong.
- The 1964 presidential election pitted Lyndon B. Johnson, a Democrat, against Republican Barry Goldwater. Even though many Americans blamed Johnson for the Gulf of Tonkin Resolution, the media portrayed Goldwater as a "war hawk" who at one point suggested the use of nuclear weapons as an option in Vietnam. This led Democrats to run the infamous **"Daisy"** commercial. The ad, which aired only once, superimposed images of a little girl plucking petals from a flower with audio of a countdown, ending in the image of a mushroom cloud. Historians credit the ad with Johnson's landslide victory.
- After President Johnson's election in 1964, he embarked on a program called **The Great Society**. This program included the 1964 **Civil Rights Act** as well as social reforms including healthcare, education, public works, and urban renewal. Part of the Great Society was Johnson's **War on Poverty**, including the Food Stamp Act, Medicare, Medicaid, Head Start, the Job Corps, and the Public Broadcasting System, among others. Critics and supporters called

these programs, "**guns and butter**." Johnson tried to balance his domestic reforms with the escalating war in Vietnam, but ultimately he was forced to siphon off funds from social programs to pay for the war.

- Johnson also faced a widening **credibility gap**, caused by conflicting reports from commanders and the reality of the war in Vietnam. While commanders would tout victories and body counts, American servicemembers and journalists were telling a different story; that America was stuck in an unwinnable war. This credibility gap led many Americans to question what, if anything, the government said that they could believe.

- The **1968 presidential conventions** held in Miami (Republican Party) and Chicago (Democratic Party) both saw protests and clashes between activists and police. Chicago saw the worst, with police using tear gas and clubs on antiwar demonstrators. In Miami, protests centered on the racial divide rather than the war. Unlike Chicago, three protestors died in clashes with Miami police.

- Richard Nixon's election in 1968 led to a shifting burden of the war onto the South Vietnamese government, with the plan being to return to the supporting role of supplying equipment and training, as well as providing economic support. The policy was called **Vietnamization** and was meant to ease the eventual withdrawal of US troops.

- **Henry Kissinger** served as Nixon's National Security Advisor, and later as Secretary of State. Kissinger engaged in peace negotiations with North Vietnam, involving China and the Soviet Union in what was called **Triangular Diplomacy**. Kissinger also held secret talks from 1969–1971 with Le Duc Tho of North Vietnam. These secret talks were an effort to move the Paris Peace Talks towards resolution.

- During the 1972 presidential race, several people were arrested after breaking into the headquarters of the Democratic Party, located inside the **Watergate** Hotel. The men were connected to the Nixon campaign, and had intended to install wiretaps and steal documents. Investigations revealed President Nixon's direct involvement with the break-in, which led Nixon to resign the presidency in August 1973.

- The 1973 **War Powers Act** passed by Congress limited the president's ability to wage war without Congressional oversight. The Act states that the resident must notify Congress within 48 hours of sending troops into any foreign country. It also requires that the president withdraw troops after 60 days unless Congress declares war or authorizes further involvement.

- Congress ended the draft in 1973, meaning that the US would have an all-volunteer military.

The Homefront

- Vietnam is considered America's first TV war. Broadcasts of fighting aired on the nightly news. This gave civilians at home an unprecedented connection to the war, and it gave American journalists the opportunity to present a more realistic image of warfare in Vietnam.
- The terms **silent majority** and **counterculture** indicated a divide not only in opinions about the Vietnam War, but also about how people chose to live. Those who lived counterculture lifestyles were called **hippies**, and were identified by their clothing, music, and slang. In contrast to the counterculture movement was the so-called "silent majority." Both President Nixon and Vice President Spiro Agnew used the term to identify those who either supported the war or chose to peacefully (and quietly) protest.
- Throughout the duration of the Vietnam War, college campuses in the US served as centers for the antiwar movement. A campus group called **The Students for a Democratic Society (SDS)** organized protests, first on campuses, then eventually to the streets of Washington, D.C. Despite their peaceful origins, the SDS did become militant, and many protests became violent clashes with police.
- As antiwar demonstrations grew beyond college campuses, an increasing number of older Americans were coming out to protest. Activists planned **Moratoria**, or mass demonstrations across the country. The largest moratorium was on October 15, 1969, where as many as two million protestors nationwide took to the streets in an effort to bring the nation to a halt.
- In May 1970, members of the Ohio National Guard were ordered to **Kent State** University to quell protestors. The Guardsmen used teargas; the protestors responded with rocks. A line of Guardsmen opened fire, killing four protestors and wounding nine more. Two days later, two protestors at Jackson State University were killed by police. Twelve others were wounded.
- The Pentagon Papers was a government study that detailed US government dishonesty regarding American involvement in Vietnam going back to the 1940s. The New York Times published a small portion of the Pentagon Papers in 1971.

Vietnam After the War

- The nation of Vietnam suffered greatly during and after the war. An estimated 2 million civilians were killed, along with 1.1 million North Vietnamese and Viet Cong soldiers. Another 250,000 South Vietnamese soldiers also died. The nation was left with many wounded and disabled people including children born with birth defects due to Agent Orange exposure. Cities, bridges, and roads were bombed to rubble; there was little food and scant medical supplies available; and agricultural areas had been destroyed by Agent Orange.

America After the War

- Following the signing of the Paris Peace Accords, North Vietnam began releasing American **prisoners of war**, first sending those with health conditions and those who had been in captivity the longest. In total, 591 POWs were released. After all the POWs had come home, the Defense Department compiled a list of 2,646 men classified as missing in action **(MIA)**. As of 2015, the remains of 1,059 servicemen had been returned to the United States for burial.

- **A Decent Interval** was a term used by Henry Kissinger, referring to his hope that South Vietnam could remain independent for a few years after the signing of the Paris Peace Accords. To Kissinger, this interval would make it appear the US had not been defeated, nor had it abandoned South Vietnam to the communists.

- Between 1964 and 1973, more than three million Americans had served in Vietnam. Of those, 47,000 were killed in combat, another 10,000 died in accidents and from other causes, and more than 150,000 had been wounded. Two thirds of those who served were volunteers. The rest were drafted. The average age of an American serviceman in Vietnam was 23 years old.

- Hispanic and African American soldiers served in disproportionate numbers; African Americans made up 11-12% of the population but accounted for 22% of those killed in Vietnam. Many Hispanic soldiers were mistakenly listed as white, but a recent study showed they made up 12% of the population but 19% of military casualties. These statistics prompted many to perceive the Vietnam War as a burden on the poor and minorities.

- Soldiers coming home from the war increasingly found themselves unwelcome in their own country. Often, returning vets were ostracized in public. Many suffered from the effects of Agent Orange exposure and **PTSD**. Because many vets were from low-income households, they struggled with unemployment and limited access to education.

- The term **Vietnam Syndrome** refers to the American foreign policy to avoid involvement in foreign wars, especially when the involvement would include ground troops. Following the US withdrawal, a **collective national amnesia** overtook the nation as talk of the war faded from public discourse.

Chapter 4

A History of the Vietnam War Post-Test

POST-TEST ANSWER SHEET

1. Ⓐ Ⓑ Ⓒ Ⓓ	15. Ⓐ Ⓑ Ⓒ Ⓓ	29. Ⓐ Ⓑ Ⓒ Ⓓ
2. Ⓐ Ⓑ Ⓒ Ⓓ	16. Ⓐ Ⓑ Ⓒ Ⓓ	30. Ⓐ Ⓑ Ⓒ Ⓓ
3. Ⓐ Ⓑ Ⓒ Ⓓ	17. Ⓐ Ⓑ Ⓒ Ⓓ	31. Ⓐ Ⓑ Ⓒ Ⓓ
4. Ⓐ Ⓑ Ⓒ Ⓓ	18. Ⓐ Ⓑ Ⓒ Ⓓ	32. Ⓐ Ⓑ Ⓒ Ⓓ
5. Ⓐ Ⓑ Ⓒ Ⓓ	19. Ⓐ Ⓑ Ⓒ Ⓓ	33. Ⓐ Ⓑ Ⓒ Ⓓ
6. Ⓐ Ⓑ Ⓒ Ⓓ	20. Ⓐ Ⓑ Ⓒ Ⓓ	34. Ⓐ Ⓑ Ⓒ Ⓓ
7. Ⓐ Ⓑ Ⓒ Ⓓ	21. Ⓐ Ⓑ Ⓒ Ⓓ	35. Ⓐ Ⓑ Ⓒ Ⓓ
8. Ⓐ Ⓑ Ⓒ Ⓓ	22. Ⓐ Ⓑ Ⓒ Ⓓ	36. Ⓐ Ⓑ Ⓒ Ⓓ
9. Ⓐ Ⓑ Ⓒ Ⓓ	23. Ⓐ Ⓑ Ⓒ Ⓓ	37. Ⓐ Ⓑ Ⓒ Ⓓ
10. Ⓐ Ⓑ Ⓒ Ⓓ	24. Ⓐ Ⓑ Ⓒ Ⓓ	38. Ⓐ Ⓑ Ⓒ Ⓓ
11. Ⓐ Ⓑ Ⓒ Ⓓ	25. Ⓐ Ⓑ Ⓒ Ⓓ	39. Ⓐ Ⓑ Ⓒ Ⓓ
12. Ⓐ Ⓑ Ⓒ Ⓓ	26. Ⓐ Ⓑ Ⓒ Ⓓ	40. Ⓐ Ⓑ Ⓒ Ⓓ
13. Ⓐ Ⓑ Ⓒ Ⓓ	27. Ⓐ Ⓑ Ⓒ Ⓓ	41. Ⓐ Ⓑ Ⓒ Ⓓ
14. Ⓐ Ⓑ Ⓒ Ⓓ	28. Ⓐ Ⓑ Ⓒ Ⓓ	42. Ⓐ Ⓑ Ⓒ Ⓓ

43. Ⓐ Ⓑ Ⓒ Ⓓ   49. Ⓐ Ⓑ Ⓒ Ⓓ   55. Ⓐ Ⓑ Ⓒ Ⓓ

44. Ⓐ Ⓑ Ⓒ Ⓓ   50. Ⓐ Ⓑ Ⓒ Ⓓ   56. Ⓐ Ⓑ Ⓒ Ⓓ

45. Ⓐ Ⓑ Ⓒ Ⓓ   51. Ⓐ Ⓑ Ⓒ Ⓓ   57. Ⓐ Ⓑ Ⓒ Ⓓ

46. Ⓐ Ⓑ Ⓒ Ⓓ   52. Ⓐ Ⓑ Ⓒ Ⓓ   58. Ⓐ Ⓑ Ⓒ Ⓓ

47. Ⓐ Ⓑ Ⓒ Ⓓ   53. Ⓐ Ⓑ Ⓒ Ⓓ   59. Ⓐ Ⓑ Ⓒ Ⓓ

48. Ⓐ Ⓑ Ⓒ Ⓓ   54. Ⓐ Ⓑ Ⓒ Ⓓ   60. Ⓐ Ⓑ Ⓒ Ⓓ

A HISTORY OF THE VIETNAM WAR POST-TEST

72 minutes—60 questions

Directions: Carefully read each of the following 60 questions. Choose the best answer to each and fill in the corresponding circle on the answer sheet. The Answer Key and Explanations can be found following this post-test.

---

1. Which of the following accurately describes how President Diem used his power?

   A. He exploited the peasants, forbade traditional religions, and enriched himself and the wealthy elite.

   B. He promised extensive land reforms, a vow that he later delivered to the surprise of the Vietnamese.

   C. He invited the US Central Intelligence Agency into South Vietnam to crush those who opposed him.

   D. He installed a puppet ruler to handle affairs of state while he partied in Europe with wealthy friends.

2. By the end of 1965, what was the approximate number of US soldiers in Vietnam?

   A. 5,000

   B. 100,000

   C. 200,000

   D. 500,000

3. The United States sent ground troops to South Vietnam in 1965

   A. as part of a UN peacekeeping force.

   B. to fight the Viet Cong insurgency.

   C. due to US popular demand.

   D. following a declaration of war by Congress.

4. What did the phrase "guns versus butter" represent to the American people of the Vietnam Era?

   A. The idea of subsidizing heavy industry or the agricultural sector

   B. A simplification of the two main areas of government funding

   C. A chant often shouted by angry protesters at antiwar marches

   D. The economics that determined if a new society would flourish

5. Why did Nixon's order to implement troop withdrawals fail to improve his overall standing with Americans?

   A. Once withdrawals began, he tried to halt them whenever he did not get his way.

   B. The withdrawals coincided with his order to increase bombing raids in Vietnam.

   C. Americans could sense that his awkward attempt to win them over was contrived.

   D. He could not shake off a bad reputation from having assisted Joseph McCarthy.

6. Which of the following factors most affected the development of religious and cultural traditions of Vietnam?

   A. Tolerance and appreciation of diversity

   B. Strict structure of Vietnamese families

   C. Vietnam's location and many resources

   D. Policy of invading surrounding regions

7. How did President Johnson gain the power to wage an undeclared war in Vietnam?

   A. He secretly met with a Supreme Court justice about revising the War Powers Act.

   B. He planted editorials in popular magazines calling for greater presidential powers.

   C. He enlisted the CIA to help stage a hoax attack to escalate American war hysteria.

   D. He used flimsy evidence to convince Congress that he needed special war powers.

8. Where did the slang term "credibility gap" first appear in 1960s culture?

   A. A folk band's song that used Buddhist philosophies to explain the evanescent nature of reality

   B. The brand name of a clothing line aimed at the youth market with "styles so real they're unreal"

   C. A senator's criticism of military officials whose reports on the war were different from the truth

   D. The name of a comedy group that used humor to expose ugly truths the government kept hidden

9. Which of the following goals did the communist forces of North Vietnam intend to accomplish with the Tet Offensive?

A. Overwhelm South Vietnam with attacks in dozens of cities then urge its people to rise up and join their victorious liberators in creating a unified communist state.

B. Launch attacks along South Vietnam's western border and begin a coordinated offensive eastward to sweep the South Vietnamese and its allies into the ocean.

C. Team up with North Vietnam's Chinese and Hmong allies into a single superior communist force that would bring all of Southeastern Asia under the communist flag.

D. Infiltrate South Vietnam's capital Saigon with thousands of North Vietnamese spies who would await the signal to destroy their enemy's government from within.

10. Which 1954 document established the neutrality of Cambodia and Laos?

A. Vientiane Agreement
B. Paris Peace Accords
C. Declaration on the Neutrality of Laos
D. Geneva Accords

11. What spurred the rise of nationalism among the Vietnamese people in the early 20th century?

A. Fascination with the 1917 communist revolution in Russia
B. Unreasonable increases in tariffs imposed by the French
C. The activism of the Vietnam Modernization Association and the Vietnam Restoration Society
D. Seeing the success of democracies in the Western world

12. Which of the following themes became a main focus of the 1964 presidential campaigns of Lyndon Johnson and Barry Goldwater?

A. The rising spirit of patriotic nationalism
B. The public's fears about nuclear weapons
C. The fight against air and water pollution
D. The government's reasons for espionage

13. Which information source helped most in introducing social and political changes of the 1960s?

A. Newspaper articles
B. Weekly newsmagazines
C. Informal newsletters
D. Televised news programs

14. What did the US military want to accomplish with its pacification program?

A. Clear out pockets of Viet Cong in the hamlets by bribing them to go back north.
B. Rebuild roads as a goodwill gesture but only in areas needing US military access.
C. Provide food and aid to Vietnamese villagers to help them resist the Viet Cong.
D. Replace negative news with positive events staged for US evening news shows.

15. Which of the following describes the situation in Vietnam during World War II?

A. Ho Chi Minh declared Vietnam a neutral territory.
B. The Vietnamese allied with the French against Japan.
C. The Vietnamese collaborated with the Japanese.
D. Bao Dai sent Vietnamese forces to aid the Soviets.

16. What was psychological warfare, and which group employed it in Vietnam? A strategy used by the

A. Viet Minh of misinformation to demoralize the South Vietnamese.
B. North Vietnamese disrupting peace talks through deceit.
C. United States of providing assistance to the Vietnamese people in hope of swaying them against communism.
D. Viet Cong of interrogation developed that included brainwashing and torture.

17. Which of the following describes the general impression the My Lai massacre incident left on Americans?

    A. US military command in Vietnam was losing control of its own troops.

    B. The United States was winning the war just as the official reports had stated.

    C. Extreme methods were necessary as modern warfare became more savage.

    D. The massacre was an isolated occurrence that affected only one unit.

18. Why did the US government direct the CIA to conduct covert operations in Laos in the early 1960s?

    A. To defend the Ho Chi Minh Trail from the Lao Thung

    B. To recruit freedom fighters from the Pathet Lao faction

    C. To train and equip Hmong tribesmen to fight communism

    D. To enforce compliance with the neutrality policy in Laos

19. Which global event set the stage for Vietnam to declare itself an independent democratic republic?

    A. The success of other democratic republics

    B. The establishment of the United Nations

    C. Europe's rebuilding of major urban areas

    D. Japan's defeat at the end of World War II

20. Which of the following was the US military's code name for its first air campaign over North Vietnam?

    A. Operation Rolling Thunder

    B. Operation Steel Tiger

    C. Operation Flaming Dart

    D. Operation 19th Parallel

21. What was the primary reason for declining African American support for Johnson prior to the election of 1968?

    A. Johnson vetoed civil rights legislation.

    B. African American soldiers served and died in disproportionate numbers in Vietnam.

    C. The African American community preferred Martin Luther King Jr. as their candidate.

    D. Johnson reversed his previous support for integrated schools.

22. What abilities did Henry Kissinger possess that made him a valuable asset to Nixon? Kissinger was a(n)

    A. diplomat in Germany with powerful political connections.
    B. skilled negotiator with a practical view of world politics.
    C. shrewd investigator who was loyal to the Republican Party.
    D. international lawyer who specialized in sensitive cases.

23. Which of the following statements describes Norodom Sihanouk's leadership of Cambodia? Sihanouk

    A. stood firm against a communist insurgency seeking to overturn Cambodia's neutrality.
    B. brokered secret deals with both communists and the United States that ultimately undermined his authority.
    C. expelled the CIA and cut diplomatic ties with the United States to gain popular support.
    D. thwarted a military coup by Lon Nol with help of the United States and North Vietnam.

24. In which way was the military strategy of the Viet Minh superior to that of the French? The Viet Minh

    A. had better military training and weapons.
    B. were skilled in guerilla warfare techniques.
    C. only needed to target white Europeans.
    D. had far greater numbers than the French.

25. When President Johnson first involved ground troops in Vietnam, how many soldiers did he send?

    A. 3,500
    B. 5,000
    C. 8,200
    D. 100,000

26. Which change in American life created difficulties for some US soldiers returning to civilian roles?

    A. Lingering division and hostility
    B. The women's liberation movement
    C. The passage of the G.I. Bill
    D. The civil rights movement

27. Which of the following terms of the Paris Peace Accords is accurate?

A. The United States would withdraw its troops and supervise the implementation of the Accords.

B. Thieu would remain president of South Vietnam until North Vietnam met the terms of the Accords.

C. North Vietnam would make no aggressive moves on South Vietnam before it held its free election.

D. An international committee would follow up after the Accords to determine the new border between North and South Vietnam.

28. Which Vietnamese intellectual led an organized resistance that threw off the domination of both France and Japan?

A. Phan Boi Chau

B. Viet Minh

C. Bao Dai

D. Ho Chi Minh

29. Which factor contributed the most to the eventual failure of the communist Tet Offensive?

A. The US military received warning through an intelligence agent to be on the alert.

B. The northern planners forgot to allow for the early arrival of the southern monsoon season.

C. The complex plan had far too many targets and insufficient numbers of troops to hold them.

D. The South Vietnamese had postponed holiday festivals during wartime and were prepared.

30. How did President Eisenhower choose to deal with the escalating trouble in French Indochina?

A. He came out against efforts to achieve independence and helped the French assert their dominion.

B. He proposed a trade war to destabilize French Indochina's economy but was vetoed by Congress.

C. He offered France aid but not US troops to avoid involving the United States in another long war.

D. He forbade the Central Intelligence Agency from engaging in covert activities in French Indochina.

31. Which of the following describes US General William Westmoreland's strategy for winning the war?

    A. Focus continual air strikes on North Vietnam's border with China to cut off Viet Cong supply lines
    B. Infiltrate the North Vietnamese Army with South Vietnamese troops to demoralize it from within
    C. Maintain a relentless ground and air offensive to kill as many North Vietnamese troops as possible
    D. Equip South Vietnamese soldiers with superior weapons and train them to defend their homeland

32. Which of the following contributed most to college campuses becoming epicenters of the antiwar movement?

    A. College towns already had social services that offered young activists resources and support.
    B. Most universities had students on deferments who organized into draft-resistance groups.
    C. Studying political science and philosophy helped inspire students to become political activists.
    D. Universities had printing departments where protesters could produce signs and pamphlets.

33. How did President Lon Nol's anticommunist agenda affect Cambodia's neutrality?

    A. Expelling North Vietnamese troops led to communist attacks that prompted a US invasion.
    B. Human rights violations led the United Nations to rescind Cambodia's neutral status.
    C. Members of Cambodian communist factions formed a coalition and sued for peace.
    D. Lon Nol petitioned for a change in Cambodia's neutral status to facilitate his plans.

34. Who used the phrase "a decent interval," and what did it mean?

    A. Gerald Ford joked about his brief stint as Nixon's vice president by calling it "a decent interval."

    B. Henry Kissinger hoped Vietnam's fragile peace would last "a decent interval" before its collapse.

    C. Congress stipulated that a president wait "a decent interval" before using the War Powers Act.

    D. A Nixon spokesman dismissed the 18-minute gap on a White House tape as "a decent interval."

35. Why was the Battle of Dien Bien Phu significant?

    A. It signaled the end of France's occupation of Vietnam.

    B. It exposed the existence of the secret Viet Minh forces.

    C. It ensured that France maintained its hold on Vietnam.

    D. It marked the first time US troops fought in Vietnam.

36. What did President Nixon provide as his reason for decreasing the number of US troops in Vietnam in 1969?

    A. The United States had won the war.

    B. The US troop morale had hit a new low.

    C. Support for the Vietnam War at home had hit a new low.

    D. The South Vietnamese Army was becoming self-sufficient.

37. US military officials measured the progress made during the war by

    A. counting the number of enemy dead after each military action.

    B. noting any change in how much ammunition the enemy was expending.

    C. keeping a daily measurement of how much territory US forces gained.

    D. monitoring reports in North Vietnamese newspapers after every battle.

38. Which of the following is the main reason that Johnson decided not to run for a second term?

A. He had been in failing health and could no longer withstand the enormous pressure of his office.

B. The recent assassinations of Martin Luther King Jr. and Robert Kennedy sickened him to the core.

C. He was weary of dealing with Vietnam and the antiwar sentiment at home.

D. The failure of his civil rights initiative had made him bitter in ways that impacted his presidency.

39. How did news footage of the moratoria change public perception of the antiwar movement?

A. It showed peaceful participants who represented a cross-section of American citizens.

B. The moratoria events helped make the peace movement into a popular media sensation.

C. Moratorium organizers hired celebrities who influenced opinion in a variety of fields.

D. Coverage of moratoria events appeared on the evening news shows during family time.

40. Which of the following is an accurate description of conditions in Vietnam ten years after Saigon fell?

A. Vietnam's economy had not recovered from the war.

B. Vietnam had begun attracting boatloads of refugees.

C. Agent Orange was no longer a problem.

D. Coffee and rice plantations jumpstarted the economy.

41. Which of the following best describes the US reports concerning the war's progress?

A. Accurate, because military analysts back at the base double checked the tally.

B. Inaccurate, because officials could not take a count during a heated battle.

C. Accurate, because officers of both sides conducted the body count together.

D. Inaccurate, because the Viet Cong didn't wear uniforms, so civilian dead often were included in the tally.

42. Which element in the Watergate Scandal most impacted the public's opinion of Richard Nixon?

A. Finding out that the president had directed members of his staff to engage in a criminal scheme

B. Watching news reports of Nixon's associates testifying about his role in the conspiracy

C. Hearing the taped discussions between the president and his advisors in the White House

D. Nixon's sudden resignation and departure from office to avoid impeachment proceedings

43. What was the biggest difference between the demonstrations at the Chicago Democratic Convention and those at the Republican Convention in Miami?

A. There were more Democratic activists than Republican activists, so the Chicago protests were larger.

B. There was less open space around Miami's convention center to accommodate protestors.

C. Chicago's protesters were focused more on the war, while the Miami demonstrations were mainly about civil rights.

D. Fewer activists lived in the conservative southern states, while the Chicago area tended to be more liberal.

44. Which radical faction rose in response to President Diem's repressive policies and acceptance of US military aid?

A. Viet Minh
B. Buddhist Liberation Front
C. Viet Cong
D. NVA

45. Which of the following was an effect of the US air campaign over North Vietnam?

A. The destruction of Saigon and Haiphong
B. Increased support for the war back home
C. Rising morale among the North Vietnamese
D. People sheltering in caves or underground

46. Which of the following describes the fate of US POWs and MIAs after the war?

A. All POWs were immediately released and the bodies of all missing troops were recovered.

B. There were substantiated reports of US soldiers living in the jungles of Vietnam after the war.

C. North Vietnam released more than 500 prisoners, but thousands of MIAs still remain unaccounted for.

D. All POWs were moved to the Hanoi Hilton to await return to the United States in comfort.

47. What is the underlying purpose of the War Powers Act?

A. To limit the chances of the United States becoming mired in a war by using military force without congressional approval

B. To allow the president to take "all necessary measures" to protect US forces

C. To define the steps in creating a formal declaration of war to ensure no critical details are missing

D. To prepare for future emergencies by adding special amendments to the presidential powers clause

48. Who was Nixon referring to when he asked for support from the "silent majority"?

A. Republicans who had not previously spoken out in support of his policies

B. Americans who supported the war in Vietnam

C. Counterculture people outside of the mainstream of American life

D. Americans who were put off by the radicalism of the antiwar left

49. Which area did President Johnson focus on in the last days of his administration?

A. Passing his final civil rights legislation

B. Trying to negotiate an end to the war

C. Regaining the American public's trust

D. Traveling to Vietnam to boost troop morale

50. Which of the following accurately describes the so-called "domino theory"?

A. US military advisors treated the conflict like it was a child's game with Vietnam as the prize.

B. The US Army focused its power by mapping out Vietnam in a south-to-north block pattern.

C. Employing subtle ways of dominating the Vietnamese would make them more cooperative.

D. If Vietnam fell to communism, other Asian nations would soon follow.

51. Which of the following is an accurate statement of the how the US military's involvement affected Vietnamese civilian life?

A. The military's advanced technology helped improve everyday life for all Vietnamese.

B. The constant bombing wiped out all of North Vietnam's cities and 60% of its farmland.

C. South Vietnamese civilians felt its impact in more ways than the North Vietnamese did.

D. North Vietnamese civilians felt its impact in more ways than the South Vietnamese did.

52. Which of the following describes North Vietnam's primary purpose in its Great Spring Offensive?

A. To demonstrate their strength

B. To announce that after waiting two years, the decent interval was over

C. To join the two Vietnams into one single unified communist state

D. To force the last remaining American holdouts to flee South Vietnam

53. Which of the following was the primary secret exposed in the Pentagon Papers?

A. The RAND Corporation's part in compiling dossiers of secret dealings in Vietnam

B. The US government's plan to blackmail antiwar activists with psychiatric records

C. The true extent of America's involvement in Vietnam

D. The US Justice Department's plan to block negative newspaper coverage of the war

54. Who was involved in the coup to remove President Diem from power, and what transpired during his takedown?

A. President Johnson concluded that Diem was a weak link in the anticommunist plan and ordered Navy SEALs to neutralize him.

B. A group of his generals, with planning assistance from the CIA, stormed the palace and assassinated Diem and his brother Nhu.

C. Military advisors who read Diem's CIA dossier considered his policies a liability to the peace process, so they had him poisoned.

D. Four Buddhist monks armed with swords ambushed Diem on his terrace and hacked him to pieces to avenge their dead fellows.

55. How effective was the US military's policy of sending recently drafted young soldiers to Vietnam and cycling them through in short deployments? It was

A. effective, because younger soldiers had more stamina to endure brutal combat conditions.

B. ineffective, because new troops did not have time to understand the Vietnamese culture.

C. effective, because older troops could not think out of the box the way younger troops did.

D. ineffective, because Vietnamese prostitutes could easily seduce young men into defecting.

56. What was Nixon's underlying rationale for his Vietnamization initiative?

A. To make the war a fight between two similar cultures so it was winnable

B. To let the United States get out of Vietnam without seeming like the loser

C. To simply reverse Johnson's plan of Americanization

D. To align with its original agreement to provide advisors but not military aid

57. Why were more than a thousand Americans still in Vietnam during the fall of Saigon? Most were

A. military deserters who waited until the US Army left.

B. embassy employees who remained after the signing of the peace agreement.

C. soldiers who were hiding from North Vietnamese invaders.

D. evacuees with nowhere to go due to the lack of available ships.

58. What effect did the assassination of President Diem have on South Vietnam?

A. South Vietnam became a contender in global politics as trading made its economy boom.

B. It freed Diem's successors to treat South Vietnamese citizens with honesty and compassion.

C. It improved life in South Vietnam by banning political corruption and human rights abuses.

D. South Vietnam suffered two years of instability as military strongmen struggled for control.

59. Which of the following was the most serious legal consequence of resisting the draft?

A. Teenagers nearing draft age sometimes developed psychological disorders.

B. Young men who evaded the draft faced the risk of arrest and imprisonment.

C. Many who had college deferments found it difficult to maintain their status.

D. Conscientious objectors were put under surveillance by police and the FBI.

60. Which of the following factors helped the Khmer Rouge gain political control in Cambodia?

A. Dissension among pro-democracy factions that increased support for the communists

B. Gaining US government support by using threats to expose its bombing in Cambodia

C. Instituting a program to attract Buddhist monks to join the Khmer Rouge as recruiters

D. The breakdown of order in Lon Nol's government as Cambodia descended into civil war

ANSWER KEY AND EXPLANATIONS

1. A	13. D	25. A	37. A	49. B
2. C	14. C	26. A	38. C	50. D
3. B	15. B	27. C	39. A	51. C
4. B	16. C	28. D	40. A	52. C
5. B	17. A	29. C	41. D	53. C
6. C	18. C	30. C	42. C	54. B
7. D	19. D	31. C	43. C	55. B
8. C	20. C	32. B	44. C	56. B
9. A	21. B	33. A	45. D	57. B
10. D	22. B	34. B	46. C	58. D
11. C	23. B	35. A	47. A	59. B
12. B	24. B	36. D	48. D	60. D

1. **The correct answer is A.** Diem's regime was marked by corruption that channeled wealth to himself and South Vietnam's upper classes, and a brutal campaign of repression against Buddhists. Diem promised land reforms (choice B) that never materialized because the wealth of the elite would have been impacted by such changes. The CIA (choice C) was an independent entity that did not operate at the behest of Diem. Bao Dai had lived the life of a playboy in Europe (choice D) until he was deposed, but Diem chose to stay in South Vietnam during his rule as president.

2. **The correct answer is C.** By the end of 1965, there were almost 200,000 American ground troops in Vietnam. The figure of 5,000 (choice A) is the number of US servicemen killed during the air campaign. In July 1965, Johnson sent 100,000 more troops (choice B). By the end of the war, there were approximately 500,000 American ground troops in Vietnam (choice D).

3. **The correct answer is B.** Diem's overthrow created a power vacuum that led to instability. The Viet Cong seized on this instability and stepped up its insurgency, prompting the United States began to commit ground troops to push back against the Viet Cong. The United Nations (choice A) did not authorize a peacekeeping force. The American public (choice C) was largely unaware of the conflict in Vietnam at this time, and the US Congress never officially declared war against North Vietnam (choice D).

4. **The correct answer is B.** Debate raged in Congress over massive budget expenditures in two areas: the US military's escalation of the war in Vietnam (the "guns") and President Johnson's Great Society plan to provide social services to the American people (the "butter").

5. **The correct answer is B.** North Vietnam had taken advantage of the withdrawals to increase its attacks, so Nixon ordered bombing runs to support the South Vietnamese military. He did not threaten to stop the withdrawals (choice A) as political leverage. He could not conceal his obvious discomfort around people (choice C), but that was not a factor here. In the early 1950s, Nixon had supported Senator Joe McCarthy's agenda (choice D) by serving as his assistant, but this was not a factor here.

6. **The correct answer is C.** Vietnam's strategic location and natural resources made it a tempting target for Chinese, Indian, and French invaders, who introduced new religions and cultural traditions throughout the region. The attitude of the Vietnamese populations regarding diversity (choice A) had little bearing on the development of religious and cultural influences. The structure of the Vietnamese family (choice B) unit did not prevent the adoption of different religions or traditions. Vietnam did not invade its neighbors (choice D) but was the target of invasion by numerous powers.

7. **The correct answer is D.** Johnson used questionable news reports and outright rumors to claim North Vietnamese forces had attacked US ships in the Gulf of Tonkin, upon which Congress passed the Gulf of Tonkin Resolution. This act granted him special war powers to "take all necessary measures" to repel attacks against US forces. Johnson did not revise the War Powers Act (choice A) to grant himself the wider power to wage war. He also did not sway public opinion with targeted editorials (choice B), nor did he use CIA agents to stage a fake attack (choice C) that would create a climate of war hysteria among the public.

8. **The correct answer is C.** Senator William Fulbright used the term "credibility gap" to describe the glaring differences between the war on paper that military officials promoted and the war on film that televised news programs showed. Young people who were opposed to the war communicated their ideas to others in the distinctive music of that era (choice A), although the band in the example is fictitious. Although the emerging youth culture began to define itself by adopting styles of dress that indicated the wearer's attitude (choice B), there was no "credibility gap" line of clothing. Comedy groups formed and performed routines that mocked authority (choice D). Although the comedy group in this example is real, the name was borrowed from Fulbright's coining of the term.

9. **The correct answer is A.** The North Vietnamese plan hoped to use the element of surprise by attacking during the Tet holiday, hoping it would spark an uprising among the South Vietnamese people and demoralize US troops and the American public. The other options (choices B, C, and D) are false but sound no less grandiose than the true plan.

10. **The correct answer is D.** The 1954 Geneva Accords were agreements regarding Cambodia and Laos that declared their neutrality and specified the restrictions. The Vientiane Agreement (choice A) was a 1973 treaty regarding a coalition government in Laos. The 1973 Paris Peace Accords (choice B) defined the terms of the agreement between North and South Vietnam to end the war. The Declaration on the Neutrality of Laos (choice C) was a 1962 agreement regarding Laos.

11. **The correct answer is C.** The rise of Vietnamese nationalism in the early 20th century was heavily influenced by Phan Boi Chau's establishment of the Vietnam Modernization Association and the Vietnam Restoration Society. Growing interest in the communist revolution in Russia (choice A) was a result of this rising discontent, not its cause. French-imposed tariff increases (choice B) were not the compelling reason for the rise of nationalistic spirit among the Vietnamese. Successful examples of Western democracy (choice D) also influenced the Vietnamese but did not cause the rise of nationalism.

12. **The correct answer is B.** The 1964 campaign was marked by nuclear bombs. Conservative senator and war hawk Barry Goldwater frequently spoke of ending the war with tactical nuclear weapons, while Lyndon Johnson feared the use of nuclear weapons might lead to the Soviet Union responding in kind, leading to World War III. The 1968 election's hot-button topic would be patriotic nationalism (choice A) as the rift deepened between war supporters and peace advocates. Fighting air and water pollution (choice B) would become a main topic in the 1970s. The covert activities of spies (choice D) would figure into politics in the 1980s.

13. **The correct answer is D.** Televised news had the greatest impact on the 1960s as trusted news anchors brought images and messages directly into millions of American homes. Through television, Americans began to feel connected to the war in a way that was not previously possible. Newspapers (choice A) and weekly newsmagazines like *Life* and *Time* (choice B) also influenced political changes, but not in as widespread way as television. Newsletters (choice C), a simple method of communication often in the form of typewritten photocopied pages sent by mail to members of small groups, were used by some activists to keep others informed of upcoming protests and political news, but were not seen by the general public.

14. **The correct answer is C.** The pacification program's objective was to "win hearts and minds" by offering South Vietnamese civilians food, medical aid, and help rebuilding in hopes of creating a bond with the United States that could make them more resistant to Viet Cong recruitment efforts. The program did not focus on bribing insurgents to leave (choice A). The main goal of the pacification program was not to rebuild roads for US military access (choice B). The program's goal was to improve relations with the Vietnamese (choice D), not silence criticism back home.

15. The correct answer is B. The Vietnamese sided with France and its allies in the fight against the Axis Powers, which included Japan. At the time, Ho had no political power and no one else moved to declare the neutrality of Vietnam in the war (choice A). The Vietnamese opposed their country's occupation by the Japanese (choice C) and thus would not choose to collaborate with them. The power of Vietnamese emperor Bao Dai was limited by the French, which meant he could not send military aid to assist other countries (choice D), much less to aid the communist Soviets.

16. The correct answer is C. The United States provided food and medical aid in hopes of increasing support for Diem and the United States, and deterring communism without violence. Though the Viet Minh used elements like surprise attacks, it did not have a plan specifically developed to break the will of their enemies (choice A). The North Vietnamese negotiators had no formal plan of psychological warfare to gain advantage in peace talks (choice B). The Viet Cong used elements like snipers and deadly traps but did not have a step-by-step plan to drive its enemies to the point of madness (choice D).

17. The correct answer is A. The shocking news gave many Americans the impression that authority had broken down and anarchy reigned among the US forces in Vietnam. Some American war hawks saw the news as proof of America's dominance (choice B), but their view was not the predominant one. Most Americans thought acts of atrocity were never justified (choice C), even in wartime. The hope was that this was an isolated incident (choice D), but other reports emerged of similar acts of atrocity that had been kept secret.

18. The correct answer is C. The CIA trained Hmong tribesmen to form an anticommunist attack force that became known as the "Secret Army." The Lao Thung (choice A) was another Laotian tribe that the CIA trained to carry out attacks on the Ho Chi Minh Trail. The Pathet Lao (choice B) was a communist faction bent on overthrowing the Laotian government. The CIA was not there to enforce the Neutrality of Laos (choice D).

19. **The correct answer is D.** The fall of Japan triggered its retreat from Japanese-occupied Vietnam, creating a political vacuum that permitted the Viet Minh to seize power. The establishment of successful democracies (choice A) elsewhere had no effect on the exchange of power in Vietnam; neither did the establishment of the United Nations (choice B). The rebuilding of major European urban centers (choice C) also had no influence over Southeast Asian affairs.

20. **The correct answer is C.** Operation Flaming Dart initiated the air campaign against North Vietnam in February 1965. Operation Rolling Thunder (choice A) was the next wave of bombing that began in March 1965. Operation Steel Tiger (choice B) was the air campaign that targeted the Ho Chi Minh Trail in Laos. There was no air campaign with the code name Operation 19th Parallel (choice D).

21. **The correct answer is B.** While black Americans represented approximately 11 percent of the total population during the war, 22 percent of the 58,000 servicemen killed in Vietnam were black. This unfair burden cost Johnson the support of many civil rights leaders, and the support of many in the African American community in general. Johnson did not veto civil rights legislation (choice A) or reverse his support for integrated schools (choice D). Instead, his Civil Rights Act of 1964 is often called the most far-reaching civil rights legislation since the Civil War. Martin Luther King Jr. (choice C) was not a presidential candidate.

22. **The correct answer is B.** Dr. Henry Kissinger was respected as a cool-headed and persuasive negotiator who understood how to craft a compromise that could appeal to all parties, making him a critical participant in the Paris Peace Talks. Kissinger was a naturalized US citizen (choice A) who had emigrated from Germany at the age of 15 and served in the US Army. Kissinger served as a geopolitical consultant and statesman, not as an investigator (choice C) or attorney (choice D).

23. **The correct answer is B.** Sihanouk's attempt to play both sides backfired when he gave North Vietnam free use of the Ho Chi Minh Trail then permitted the US government to conduct bombing raids on the Trail, causing civilian deaths and throwing Cambodia into turmoil. Sihanouk adopted an anticommunist stance to gain US support against his communist rivals the Khmer Rouge while willingly protecting communist North Vietnam's interests in Cambodia (choice A). Sihanouk was motivated by his fear that the CIA was plotting against him (choice C) rather than by a desire to increase his approval rating. Sihanouk's government was overthrown by Lon Nol's forces (choice D) when he was out of the country.

24. **The correct answer is B.** The French used conventional methods of warfare suited for Europe, while the Viet Minh used guerilla techniques suited for Vietnam, fighting in small units from the concealment of the jungle, giving the Viet Minh a powerful tactical advantage. But the Viet Minh had few weapons and very little military training (choice A). The Viet Minh's enemy was not exclusively white and European (choice C) because the French used Vietnamese colonial troops to do much of the fighting. The Viet Minh outnumbered French troops (choice D), but their greater numbers were no advantage against the superior armaments of the French forces.

25. **The correct answer is A.** The first deployment of US soldiers numbered 3,500 troops. The figure of 5,000 (choice B) is the number of US servicemen killed during the air campaign. By June 1965, a total of 8,200 troops (choice C) had been sent. In July 1965, Johnson sent 100,000 more troops (choice D).

26. **The correct answer is A.** Many soldiers came back psychologically shattered by their experiences in Vietnam only to become targets of protesters angered by reports of brutal acts committed by US soldiers, such as at My Lai. While the women's liberation and the civil rights movements (choices B and D), brought changes to society in general, they did not cause difficulties for veterans in particular. The G.I. Bill (choice C), which was passed in 1944, helped veterans by offering them educational opportunities and other benefits.

27. The correct answer is C. The North Vietnamese government had to show good faith by making no aggressive moves on South Vietnam before its government held free elections. An international committee would oversee the implementation of the Accords (choice A), not the United States. The terms dictated that Thieu would be president until South Vietnam held its free elections, not until North Vietnam had fulfilled its terms (choice B). The Accords defined the border between North and South Vietnam as the 17th parallel (choice D).

28. The correct answer is D. Ho Chi Minh, founder of Vietnam's Communist Party, marshalled the Vietnamese citizens into an effective resistance movement opposing the domination of imperialist nations over Vietnam. Phan Boi Chau (choice A) and his Vietnam Modernization Association also opposed French rule but sought Japanese support to overthrow the French. Viet Minh (choice B) was the name of Ho's forces that opposed the Japanese occupation of Vietnam. Bao Dai (choice C) was Vietnam's last reigning emperor who abdicated in 1945 when Vietnam was officially declared a democratic republic.

29. The correct answer is C. The number of troops required to attack multiple targets at once was far greater than the North Vietnamese could marshal. Its forces had to spread out so much that it weakened their ability to be the aggressors. The offensive was a surprise to the US troops (choice A), but they easily rallied and counterattacked the smaller communist forces. There was no monsoon (choice B), and the Tet celebration was not cancelled (choice D).

30. The correct answer is C. Eisenhower well remembered experiencing heavy combat in World War II and knew American citizens would oppose their country entering another war so soon, so he offered France extensive financial aid but no military support. Though he supported the French, he did not condemn the Vietnamese independence movement (choice A). He did not start a trade war (choice B) with the intention of ruining French Indochina's economy. Eisenhower approved of using the CIA (choice D) in Vietnam to help install Ngo Ninh Diem as president in order to prevent communists from seizing power.

31. The correct answer is C. Westmoreland believed that using an unlimited number of US troops to kill off the enemy with constant bombing runs and ground assaults would force North Vietnam to surrender by 1967. He focused on cutting off North Vietnam's supply lines to the Viet Cong (choice A) along the Ho Chi Minh Trail and the border with South Vietnam. Westmoreland considered the South Vietnamese troops unable to mount a strong offensive or provide an adequate defense for its homeland (choices B and D).

32. The correct answer is B. College students did not want to be drafted into a war they didn't support once they graduated. Beyond that, however, the antiwar movement on college campuses represented change in how young people perceived the role of the United States in the world. College towns did have social services available (choice A), but many communities often did not support the antiwar activities. Studying political science (choice C) and philosophy may have helped students understand their own positions, but studying these topics did not create an impetus for the antiwar movement. Access to printing departments was an advantage but not the main reason for the movement (choice D).

33. The correct answer is A. Expelling North Vietnamese troops and shutting down access to the Ho Chi Minh Trail prompted the North Vietnamese to move deeper into Cambodia, which in turn led the United States to invade Cambodia as well. The United Nations did not rescind Cambodia's neutrality (choice B). The communist factions did not unite to sue Lon Nol for peace (choice C) but rather to support North Vietnam's retaliation against its expulsion. Lon Nol could not dictate changes in the neutral agreement of Cambodia (choice D).

34. The correct answer is B. Kissinger knew Vietnam's existence as an independent state was fated to be short, but he noted his hope it would last "a decent interval" of two or three years to lessen the perception that the United States had abandoned South Vietnam to the communists.

35. **The correct answer is A.** The defeat of the French at the Battle of Dien Bien Phu ended their imperial authority in Vietnam. The existence of the Viet Minh (choice B) had been known since the 1940s. Losing the pivotal battle made the French decide to leave Vietnam (choice C) instead of engaging in an expensive war to retain its control. The battle was between the French and Vietnamese forces (choice D) without involving the use of US military troops.

36. **The correct answer is D.** Nixon declared that large numbers of US troops were no longer needed because the South Vietnamese Army had done much of the work to push back the attacking North Vietnamese Army during the Tet Offensive. Nixon was also looking for a rationalization for his real goal, which was to improve his own political standing at home with a public that was increasingly antiwar (choice C). Although US troop morale was low (choice B), that was not Nixon's justification for decreasing the number of US troops. The United States had not won the war (choice A).

37. **The correct answer is A.** After engaging in combat, officers would count the number of enemy dead bodies left on the battle site and report the figures to Central Command. There was no attempt to track the amount of ammunition used by the enemy (choice B). Since territory was repeatedly gained and lost and regained again, it was impossible to track the progress on maps (choice C). Any news coming from North Vietnam (choice D) was regarded as propaganda and not the truth.

38. **The correct answer is C.** Though Lyndon Johnson had been a relentless campaigner who refused to back down under opposition, the pressures of his presidency had worn him down, especially following the Tet Offensive. Johnson saw the rising tide of antiwar sentiment when antiwar candidate Eugene McCarthy placed a strong second in the New Hampshire primary. He opted to finish his term focusing on arranging peace talks to end the war. Johnson's health (choice A) was not the motivating factor. Though the murders of King and Kennedy (choice B) no doubt caused him concern, they were not the reason he refused to run. Far from failing, Johnson's landmark 1964 Civil Rights Act (choice D) was a pivotal success that led to widespread social reforms.

39. **The correct answer is A.** Many older middle-class Americans did not identify with campus protests. However, the image of thousands of people like themselves all demonstrating peacefully at moratoria led a wider variety of people to rethink their positions on the war. The public interest generated by the moratoria was directed toward creating awareness, not media popularity (choice B). The well-known people (choice C), such as Dr. Benjamin Spock, who spoke at moratoria were not hired but were actual supporters of the antiwar movement who were willing to add their names to the cause. The time the coverage appeared (choice D) affected the number of viewers but did not increase their feelings of identification with the demonstrators.

40. **The correct answer is A.** Vietnam's economy remained depressed until 1986 when economic reforms began to stimulate trade and industry. The boats (choice B) were full of Vietnamese refugees fleeing their country, not hopeful immigrants arriving in Vietnam. After ten years, the chemicals in Agent Orange (choice C) had largely broken down, but the birth defects it had caused continue to impact the lives of countless survivors of the war. The economic boost from coffee and rice exports (choice D) occurred in modern-day Vietnam.

41. **The correct answer is D.** The fact that the Viet Cong didn't wear uniforms led to highly inaccurate counts as the bodies of villagers and peasants were frequently misidentified as NVA troops or Viet Cong insurgents. Other factors also contributed to inaccuracy, such the fact that the Viet Cong did have resources to remove their dead from the field, which caused them to be counted again in subsequent battles. Military analysts (choice A) who had not been on the scene could not tell if reporting officers had made mistakes or deliberately inflated their figures. Counts were conducted after a battle was over (choice B), not during the action. Officials from both sides did not conduct tallies of the dead together (choice C).

42. **The correct answer is C.** Hearing the White House tapes of President Nixon's private conversations that implicated him in the break-in and in which he revealed his vindictive, spiteful, and venal nature. Other aspects of the Watergate Scandal (such as choices A, B, and D) also influenced opinion, but hearing Nixon condemn himself in his own voice had the greatest impact.

43. **The correct answer is C.** The Chicago Democratic Convention attracted thousands of antiwar protesters from around the country, while the Miami demonstrators wanted to draw attention to the poor living conditions and lack of opportunities in Liberty City, the largest black neighborhood in Miami. Political party affiliation (choice A) was not the biggest difference between the demonstrations. The amount of space available (choice B) for staging demonstrations was not a factor in crowd size. The conservative climate of the South did not impact the turnout, nor did the liberal climate of Chicago (choice D).

44. **The correct answer is C.** The Viet Cong (or National Liberation Front) was an anti-Diem communist guerilla force organized to oppose South Vietnam government forces and, later, fight the US military. The Viet Minh (choice A) was the group organized by Ho Chi Minh to oppose the Japanese in the 1940s. There was no group called the Buddhist Liberation Front (choice B). The NVA (choice D, also known as the North Vietnamese Army), which sometimes acted with the Viet Cong, was the military force in the communist-held north.

45. **The correct answer is D.** Many fearful North Vietnamese civilians sought protection in caves or underground hiding places they had dug out. Unlike Haiphong, Saigon is not in North Vietnam (choice A). The escalating war in Vietnam increased the outrage at home (choice B), resulting in bigger protest marches and more American voices calling for an end to the war. North Vietnam's claims that the bombings had increased morale among its populations (choice C) were false propaganda.

46. The correct answer is C. Over several weeks following the signing of the peace agreements, North Vietnam released 591 U.S POWs (choice A). However, of the 2,646 soldiers listed as missing in action in Vietnam, Cambodia, and Laos, 1,588 are still MIA. While there were rumors of US soldiers living in the jungle (choice B), these claims were never substantiated. The "Hanoi Hilton" (choice D) was the nickname given to an infamous North Vietnamese prison by US troops held captive there, where they were tortured and deprived of food, sleep, and light.

47. The correct answer is A. The act's aim is to prevent another situation like Vietnam in which the United States was trapped in an undeclared war for two decades, with the president conducting the war almost singlehandedly. Allowing the president to use whatever means necessary to prevent attack against US forces (choice B) was part of the Tonkin Gulf Resolution, which the War Powers Act was meant to rescind. The War Powers Act does not define the drafting of a declaration of war (choice C). There are no special amendments in the War Powers Act (choice D).

48. The correct answer is D. Nixon believed that the vast majority of Americans disapproved of the actions of antiwar radicals. He felt that most of the people supported him, but were not speaking out. Not all the people in Nixon's silent majority were Republicans (choice A), nor did all of them support the war (choice B). Even some people who opposed the war were put off by the radicalism of the antiwar movement (choice C). People considered "counter-culture" were, in Nixon's eyes, the opposite of the silent majority.

49. The correct answer is B. Lyndon Johnson spent his final weeks as president working on ways to get the North Vietnamese government to agree to meet representatives of South Vietnam to discuss the possibility of forging a peace agreement. His civil rights legislation (choice A) had already passed. He did not try to restore his reputation with the American public (choice C) as it would have been a waste of time in the heated atmosphere of protests and demonstrations. He did not travel to Vietnam at that time (choice D).

50. **The correct answer is D.** Halting the spread of communism was the main reason the US government got involved in Vietnam. US military advisors understood the seriousness of the Vietnam War (choice A) and did not regard it as a mere game. They learned fast that the strategy of focusing their firepower in an orderly section-by-section sweep (choice B) could not quell a widespread conflict. The domino theory was not about the domination of the Vietnamese (choice C).

51. **The correct answer is C.** In North Vietnam, civilian populations mainly suffered bombardments from the skies without ground assault, while South Vietnam was the scene of many ground battles. Also, US troops had trouble distinguishing the Viet Cong from civilians, leading to civilian casualties. South Vietnamese civilians also faced persecution by the Viet Cong, who confiscated their rice and cattle and conscripted civilians to build tunnels. The US technological advances mainly involved weaponry, aircraft, and communications (choice A), which offered few improvements suited to Vietnam's agrarian economy. Although bombing was heavy in North Vietnam (choice D), it did not experience the ground battles that South Vietnam did.

52. **The correct answer is C.** The creation of a unified communist state and the related capture of Saigon fueled the Great Spring Offensive. While a show of strength (choice A) is an aspect of most military actions, it wasn't the main purpose of the Great Spring Offensive. Kissinger had hoped South Vietnam would last two to three years, but his "decent interval" (choice B) was not part of the terms of the Paris Peace Accords. Forcing the last Americans out of Vietnam (choice D) was not the purpose of the offensive but an effect of it.

53. **The correct answer is C.** The Pentagon Papers detailed how presidents as far back as Truman had failed to be honest about the extent of US involvement in Vietnam and concealed the truth from the American people. The RAND Corporation (choice A) conducted the study and employed the whistleblower Daniel Ellsberg. The US government broke into the office of Ellsberg's psychiatrist (choice B) to steal his files in an attempt to discredit him. The Justice Department had tried to stop publication of the Pentagon Papers in the *New York Times* (choice D) but the US Supreme Court sided with the media.

54. **The correct answer is B.** A group of South Vietnamese Army generals staged a coup, assassinating Diem and his brother Ngo Dinh Nhu. The US Central Intelligence Agency (CIA) helped plan the coup, though it's likely the US government did not want them to go so far as to have Diem assassinated, fearing that would make him a martyr. Diem's assassination did not involve US forces (choice A). Diem was murdered in the coup, but not poisoned (choice C). Though some Buddhist monks committed suicide by self-immolation, they were nonviolent (choice D) and did not attack Diem.

55. **The correct answer is B.** Inexperienced young soldiers were plunged into an entirely unfamiliar foreign land full of people whose culture and language seemed unfathomable, where their short tour of duty left them insufficient time to learn how to interpret important clues that often were critical to their survival. While fresh troops had the energy to withstand the demands of warfare (choice A), their lack of combat experience increased their chances of becoming battlefield casualties. Experienced soldiers with multiple deployments were seasoned fighters who understood warfare (choice C), but the new men on short deployments that they were leading were often more focused on going home instead of final victory. Though there were US military deserters, the greater percentage of young recruits found it far easier to defect to neutral countries like Canada and Sweden before they were deployed to Vietnam (choice D).

56. **The correct answer is B.** Nixon wanted to end the ongoing protests and unrest by getting the US military out of Vietnam, but he did not want the world powers to think the United States was fleeing and leaving South Vietnam defenseless. The idea that the war could be resolved more easily if the United States was removed from the dynamic (choice A) was not the motivation for getting out. Nixon did not simply reverse Johnson's plan (choice C). Aligning with the original agreement to provide advisors (choice D) was an excuse that was suggested but not the real reason.

57. The correct answer is B. The United States maintained an embassy once the Paris Peace Accords were signed. Employees of the US Embassy remained at their posts and assisted in the final evacuations, which included 7,000 Vietnamese civilians. The number of military deserters (choice A) who blended in with the evacuees is unknown, as is the number who might have been in hiding (choice C). Saigon was chaotic and crowded during the invasion, but almost all Americans were safely evacuated (choice D).

58. The correct answer is D. The struggle for control over South Vietnam brought a series of corrupt military generals who struggled to gain control. Vietnam was not a global political power (choice A), nor did the nation see economic recovery until 1986. Diem's successors did not start treating citizens with respect or compassion (choice B). Rather than eliminate corruption and human rights abuses (choice C), the coup brought more.

59. The correct answer is B. The Selective Service's mandate required men ages 18–45 to register for the draft. Those who sought to evade the draft faced arrest and imprisonment. Many young men facing the draft experienced such dread and fear that the tension sometimes manifested as anxiety disorders (choice A), a serious consequence, but not a legal one. Deferments for college students were temporary and came with strict requirements in order to maintain them (choice C), but by 1970, the number of men seeking exemptions outnumbered those drafted. It was not the standard policy to place all conscientious objectors under surveillance (choice D).

60. The correct answer is D. The Khmer Rouge took advantage of widespread unrest and political instability to seize power in Cambodia. Gains it could make from political infighting (choice A) paled when compared with the power vacuum left by civil war. The Khmer Rouge did not become powerful by blackmailing the United States (choice B) over its secret bombing. The Khmer Rouge were anti-religion, especially where Buddhists were concerned (choice C).

Like what you see? Get unlimited access to Peterson's full catalog of DSST practice tests, instructional videos, flashcards, and more for **75% off the first month!** Go to **www.petersons.com/testprep/dsst** and use coupon code **DSST2020** at checkout. Offer expires July 1, 2021.

Printed in the USA
CPSIA information can be obtained
at www.ICGtesting.com
JSHW012039140824
68134JS00033B/3143

9 780768 944556